HOW TO LET GOD SOLVE YOUR PROBLEMS

GREAT
COMMISSION
MEDIA

My soul, wait thou only upon God;
for my expectation is from him.
He only is my rock and my salvation:
He is my defence;
I shall not be moved.
Psalm 62:5-6, KJV

Dr. Charles F. Stanley

HOW TO LET GOD SOLVE YOUR PROBLEMS

Discovering His Truth and
Hope for Your Life

Published in Atlanta, Georgia, by Great Commission Media, LLC.

All Scripture quotations, unless otherwise noted, are taken from the NEW AMERICAN STANDARD BIBLE®, Copyright © 1960, 1962, 1963, 1968, 1971, 1972, 1973, 1975, 1977, 1995 by The Lockman Foundation. Used by permission.

ISBN: 0-9770976-4-1

Requests for information should be addressed to:
Great Commission Media
P.O. Box 548
Lebanon, GA 30146

To discover other Charles Stanley teaching resources, visit www.charlesstanleyinstitute.com or www.intouch.org

CONTENTS

The difficulties that the apostle Paul faced were anything but light. He tells us, "Five times I received from the Jews thirty-nine lashes. [Forty lashes was a sentence of sure death.] Three times I was beaten with rods, once I was stoned, three times I was shipwrecked, a night and a day I have spent in the deep. I have been on frequent journeys, in dangers from rivers, dangers from robbers, dangers from my countrymen, dangers from the Gentiles, dangers in the city, dangers in the wilderness, dangers on the sea, dangers among false brethren; I have been in labor and hardship, through many sleepless nights, in hunger and thirst, often without food, in cold and exposure. Apart from such external things, there is the daily pressure on me of concern for all the churches. Who is weak without my being weak? Who is led into sin without my intense concern? If I have to boast, I will boast of what pertains to my weakness. The God and Father of the Lord Jesus, He who is blessed forever" (2 Corinthians 11:24-31).

From a human perspective, Paul should have been

dead, but he was alive to do the will of God. He writes, "For even when we came into Macedonia our flesh had no rest, but we were afflicted on every side: conflicts without, fears within. But God, who comforts the depressed, comforted us" (2 Corinthians 7:5-6). Here is the wondrous truth of God: when you face sorrow, heartbreak, and disappointment, He will do the same for you. He will comfort you so that you will learn to drink deeply of His love and desire to walk in the light of His mercy and grace every day. Not only this, but as the winds of adversity blow across your life, He will teach you and prepare you to be a comforter of others.

The problem you are facing today may be one that has lingered long—so long that you wonder when the storm will subside and life will return to normal. Adversity, pain, and trouble change us and when God is involved, the change always leads to future blessing and eternal hope.

Based on God's eternal faithfulness, I want to challenge you *never* to give up but to do what Joseph, Elijah, Moses, Paul, and Peter, as well as many others did. They stayed the course, fought the good fight, and developed a new attitude toward the problems they faced. They realized that when

God allows difficulty, He always has a greater plan in mind. The difficulty you are facing today will vanish in His presence because He is the One who solves every problem you have. He will calm your fears and provide the hope and instruction you need to face tomorrow.

This is His promise to all who believe and place their trust in Him. It is my prayer that you will come to know the love of the Savior in such a deep and abiding way that when life turns dark and stormy, you immediately will turn to Him in prayer and watch in amazement as He works on your behalf. He has never failed to keep a single promise. Therefore, watch, believe, and know that if adversity has touched your life, He is at work and He will bring you through this season of difficulty victoriously!

Charles F. Stanley
Atlanta, Ga.

CHAPTER ONE

No Problem Too Great

Nothing was gentle or kind about Hurricane Katrina. What began as a small tropical storm on August 24, 2005, quickly became a category one hurricane as it passed just north of Key West, Florida. At the time, no one would have thought that in less than four days, this storm would turn into a raging category five hurricane with wind speeds surpassing 170 mph, but this is exactly what it did.

After frightening residents of Key West and chasing tourists away from the southern most point of the US, the storm turned northward and headed out into the Gulf of Mexico where warmer than normal water temperatures awaited its arrival and fueled its growing fury. Two days later, weather forecasters were stunned by the satellite images they were receiving detailing the storm's track. At one point, the hurricane, along with its outer rain bands, completely filled the Gulf of Mexico. Even more frightening was the fact that the hurricane had trained its eye on the coastal areas of Louisiana, Mississippi, and the western third of Alabama.

Residents began frantically packing cars and seeking any route of escape. Highways quickly became slow moving parking lots as people fled from the inevitable. Countless others, however, believed they could outlast the storm on their own. Some said they had no way to leave the area. They boarded up their houses or sought refuge in shelters but to little avail. As Katrina approached land, local government officials realized this storm would be physically, emotionally, and mentally devastating to everyone in its path. Destruction would be mammoth and recovery would not be easy or quick.

Just as it made landfall, Hurricane Katrina weakened to a category four, but its sustained winds hovered at 145 mph, and Americans witnessed one of the most deadly and costly storms in history plow ashore. Close to 1,300 people died in storm-related deaths and damage estimates reported to be more than 200 billion dollars. More than a million people were displaced from their homes. Countless individuals were separated from loved ones and the question on everyone's mind seemed to be: how could this have happened?

Winds of Adversity

The winds of adversity blow strong. They also blow in every direction. They do not discriminate between rich or poor—weak or strong. Though many people try desperately to avoid difficulty and hardship, sooner or later adversity strikes each of our lives. No one is exempt from sorrow, heartache, disappointment, and even tragedy. When adversity does hit, and especially if we lose our focus on Christ, it can cause a multitude of problems: fear, anxiety, and anger. It can tempt us to doubt God's goodness and to feel as though the very foundation of our lives will crumble away.

In the aftermath of a storm—whether it is emotional or physical—we may be tempted to wonder if we will ever be able to put the pieces of our lives back together. After all, how do we recoup from the heartfelt loss of our home and family or that of a friend, the death of a spouse, or the sharp and painful feelings that come as a result of divorce? How can we go on after hearing the news that we have been let go from a job we loved? Will we ever get past the stinging reality of finding out that the husband or wife who once vowed to love until "death do us part" loves someone else? Is there any cure for the feelings of loneliness, isolation, and depression we are feeling? Will life ever return to a normal pace after suffering a long and serious illness? The answer to these questions is found through our faith in God. In the aftermath of any storm, He is the only One we can turn to for the encouragement we need to carry on each day.

Often we search through the debris of our lives looking for signs of hope and anything still connected to the life we once knew. However, even if everything we once regarded as familiar changes, God remains the same (Hebrews 13:8). He is our eternal anchor of hope in stormy and difficult times (Hebrews 6:19). And, He has promised never to forsake those who love Him (Deuteronomy 31:6, 8; Hebrews 13:5).

You may be thinking, "My life has been shattered, and

I just don't believe there is any hope within me. I got up this morning, went to my office, and a few minutes later, my manager told me the company no longer needed me. Suddenly, I realized that I had been fired and now I feel numb and wonder what I will do to take care of my family."

There are seasons to life—times when the winds of adversity can hit without warning but with the force of a category five hurricane. These are the very moments when we may not understand why difficulty has touched our lives. At first thought, we may wonder what we have done so wrong to have our lives impacted with so much hurt. We also can languish in feelings of denial believing that whatever has happened will just up and go away, but after a few days and weeks, we realize that whatever has touched our lives really did take place.

There are countless examples of storm-driven moments. I often tell those in my congregation that if a person lives long enough, he or she will experience some type of adversity. This is not a negative way to look at life, but one that is realistic. Being prepared for seasons of difficulty gives us the wisdom we need to rationally examine a problem when it comes and to be more willing to turn it over the Lord rather than succumb to feelings of depression, guilt, or shame.

More than likely, you know what it feels like to face sorrow or disappointment. For the person who has picked up this book with the hope of finding an answer to the heaviness he or she is feeling, there is great news: God has promised restoration. He tells us in Joel 2:25, "I will make up to you for the years that the swarming locust has eaten, the creeping locust, the stripping locust and the gnawing locust." God knows when we face difficulties that are beyond our ability to handle them. He also promises hope and restoration when our faith is in Him alone. In Deuteronomy 30:1-3, He says, "So it shall be when all of these things have come upon you, the blessing and the curse which I have set before you, and you call them to mind . . . and you return to the Lord your God and obey Him with all your heart and soul . . . then the Lord your God will restore you."

The Lord is the One who provides the strength and the courage we need to go forward by faith, trusting Him with our future even when the sun does not appear for many days and months. He is not the author of evil, nor did His original design include devastation and heartache. However, He uses both of these for His purpose, glory, and our blessing.

Adversity is a deep rich color of love and divine care that He weaves into the fabric of our lives. Nothing touches us without first passing through Him. He also selects threads of joy and blessing to blend into His design. When God allows adversity to strike our lives, He does so with the full intent of using it for a greater blessing. Through times of extreme difficulty, He develops our godly character, strengthens us spiritually, and helps us grow deeper in our faith in Him. A young missionary told how she had faced many difficulties over the past year of her ministry in a spiritually dark foreign country. She was living life right in the center of God's will. Yet, she began facing one sleepless night after another. Was she worried about the circumstances of her life? No. Was she involved in some type of entangling sin—absolutely not! The enemy was attacking her and tempting her to think that perhaps God had abandoned her, but nothing was further from the truth.

Do you remember what God said to Satan concerning Job? He asked the enemy, "Have you considered My servant Job? For there is no one like him on the earth, a blameless and upright man, fearing God and turning away from evil" (Job 1:8). At times adversity strikes because you are doing exactly what God wants you to do. Job was right in the middle of God's will. Not only that, he was a godly man who feared the Lord and was blameless and upright. Yet, God allowed the winds of adversity to blow through his life with such a force that it left Job crying and wondering if he could continue living. Even with one tragedy befalling him after another, Job refused to blame God. "Naked I came from my mother's womb, and naked I shall return there. The Lord gave and the Lord has taken away. Blessed be the name of the Lord" (Job 1:21). The Bible goes on to say, "Through all this Job did not sin nor did he blame God" (v. 22).

At times a storm can appear devastating, but it also can open the door to new possibilities in ways that we have never considered. How can this be true, especially when it comes to dealing with the death of a loved one or some other cherished loss? Adversity comes as a result of two different aspects.

It often strikes as a result of living in a fallen environment. While God originally created this world to be perfect, Adam and Eve sinned and we are now living with the consequences of their disobedience. We also experience adversity when we fail to obey God. All sin has consequences—some much more serious than others. While the consequences of sin are very serious, God never stops loving us and when we acknowledge our need of Him and that we have made a wrong turn, He is quick to restore our fellowship with Himself.

Always A Reason for Hope

There is always hope with God—always room for His mercy and grace to be demonstrated. You may think that in your disobedience you have gone too far. Nothing is beyond His reach—no sin too great for Him to handle. He is God; He is sovereign, and He loves you with an infinite love. Many times, He may allow adversity to strike in order to turn you back to Himself.

In their agony, Adam and Eve cried out and the Lord moved on their behalf. Though He cast them out of the garden of Eden, He made garments for them to wear (Genesis 3:21). He also set into motion His plan of redemption for you and me, which included the coming of His Son, the Savior of the World. The Bible tells us, "For God so loved the world [you] that He gave His only begotten Son, that whoever believes in Him shall not perish, but have eternal life" (John 3:16).

God is greater than any form of evil this world could ever produce. He is alive and present with us through the power of His Holy Spirit in the lives of those who have accepted Jesus Christ as Savior and Lord. This means that not only do we have a sure hope for what seems to be the most hopeless of circumstances, we also have a loving Savior, who comforts us in our times of trial and heartache (2 Corinthians 1:3-4).

He has a plan for your life even if it has been damaged and torn apart by the winds of adversity (Jeremiah 29:11). You may think that there is no way He could ever love you, but He does. He created you in love for the purpose of knowing and loving you.

Some of the problems we face are *not* the result of anything we did. Catastrophic events that involve innocent people are not the result of anything we have done wrong. God is not a stern judge who is sitting up in heaven waiting for the right moment to crush us for our actions.

He is a God of love but when we make unwise decisions, He allows us to face the consequences of these wrong choices. Adam disobeyed God, and therefore, suffered for failing to do what God has commanded Him to do. When we violate a principle of God, we can expect to suffer some type of adversity. Many times, we are quick to recognize what we have done and take the right steps to correct the situation. Other times, we may not be as quick to respond correctly and the adversity intensifies until we respond to God's correction.

There are always consequences to sin. An action that we are sure will not hurt anyone, does. Words can be thoughtlessly spoken so as to bring deep hurt to a person's life. We may casually dismiss our actions as being done in fun, but God thinks differently and will prick our conscience until we acknowledge that what we have done is wrong.

A few years ago, I sat in my office listening to a young man who had come by the church to drop off a few things. He ended up asking to see me. After a few minutes of light conversation, I suddenly became aware that storm clouds were not only building in this man's life, they were breaking open. He said that he did not think he could go on with his marriage. He was visibly nervous and I knew something was sincerely wrong. Then he admitted that he was seeing another woman. He was a young man in his early 30's who was married and had two children. The situation had escalated to a point where he was considering leaving his wife.

When he first became involved with the other woman, he falsely believed that he would not hurt anyone but himself. But the rippling effects of his sin quickly proved him wrong as members of his immediate and extended family expressed shock and outrage.

"How did I let this go so far?" he asked through tears of frustration. "I could lose all that I have and all that I love." His question was all too familiar. Over the years, I had heard others ask the same thing, and I always wondered how the enemy is so able and ready to set up shop and gain such a sturdy foothold in a strong believer's life.

When we think about stormy situations, we usually believe these include storms such as an unexpected sickness, an unforeseen financial distress, or an unpreventable accident. This is true, but many of the storms we face also come as the result of personal sin—sin that could have been prevented by just saying no to a single thought of temptation. My friend had a lot of work to do before he could experience the unconditional love and trust of his family once again. However, he was able to make it because he sought forgiveness and refuge in Christ. With God's help, he was able to turn away from the sin that almost destroyed his family.

What type of storm you are facing today? Do you realize that even if it has appeared as a result of something you have done that God is in it with you? You are never alone. He will not forsake you when you call to Him and admit that you failed to follow His principles and need His forgiveness and wisdom in order to right what has been done wrong. He is your unshakable refuge and though you may have strayed, He will restore you when you turn your heart back to Him.

Someone Who Understands

With this in mind, how do you handle adversity? What do you do when the walls of your life collapse and there seems to be no point of retreat for you? How do you go on to face the next day and the day after that?

In the back of the lonely, dark cave of Adullam, David's tears ran heavy down his face. He had never been in a place like this one. Sure, he had been on the battlefield facing fierce soldiers of war, but never here and certainly never alone. Alone! That is the way he felt. Though four hundred men were with him, he felt alone and the pain he experienced was horrifying. (1 Samuel 22:1)

How did this happen? Wasn't he the anointed king of Israel? Didn't he have a secure place to live, a home in Jerusalem, and friends who opened their lives to him? There was nothing in this place to welcome him except a handful of sandy soil and the constant dripping of seeping water emerging from the rocky walls that concealed him from his enemy—King Saul.

When David bowed for Samuel to anoint him king, he had no idea his life was headed for turmoil and trouble. In fact, more than likely, he imagined triumph and victory. Instead, he found himself writing these few words of a prayer and psalm to God, "Be gracious to me, O God, be gracious to me, for my soul takes refuge in You; and in the shadow of Your wings I will take my refuge until destruction passes by. I will cry to God Most High, to God who accomplishes all things for me. He will send from heaven and save me" (Psalm 57:1-3).

No matter how painful your situation may be, God has a greater purpose in mind for the heartache that you are suffering. Over the weeks, months, and even years that followed, those few moments spent in a cave of discouragement were never forgotten by David. He had learned a simple principle—one that would rule His life: trust God with your circumstances and leave all the consequences to Him. He was molding David's life for a greater challenge and a greater blessing. He had a plan in mind for the disappointments His servant faced, just as He does for us.

Perhaps, the winds of adversity are blowing hard against your life. You tell your friends that you feel numb and defeated. God, however, wants you to lift your head so you can see the many promises, opportunities, and blessings He has waiting for you.

The Wrong View

There is a popular religious view in our world today that is totally opposite to what the Bible teaches. It tells us that if we will trust God, believe in Him, and make sure our faith is focused in the right direction then we will never have to face adversity. Nothing could be further from the truth. The fact is that during our lifetime, each one of us will face many trials. Some will be simple to weather, while others will be much more difficult. Having the wrong view of adversity can lead to serious problems. This can cause us to doubt God when we need to buckle down and trust Him to an even greater degree. It also can tempt us to become cynical and bitter, especially when we adopt a "poor me" attitude.

Whenever you face adversity, ask God to help you understand His will and purpose for the difficulty. He may not give you a well-outlined reason, but over time, you will begin to understand that even during seasons of deep sorrow, there is an unquenchable light of hope burning within the heart of God. His Light always shines in the darkness (John 1:5). It burns for each one of us who dare to trust Him to take us beyond the heartache to a place of healing and restoration.

One of the surest ways to come face-to-face with this hope is to begin by reading the Word of God. The theme of His unconditional love and restoration is woven throughout the very fabric of the Bible. It is not a book of judgment; it is a book that chronicles the amazing, unconditional love of a holy and righteous God, who loves you with an everlasting love. Within its pages, you will discover that you are not alone when you face sorrow and difficulty. Each one of the saints of God faced times of tremendous trial and discouragement. They struggled with feelings of fear and thoughts of defeat. However, they were relentless in their faith because they were convinced that the One who promised to deliver from heartache would do it, and He did. The awesome truth is that He is willing to do the same for you and me today.

CHAPTER TWO

Never Give Up!

I have been a Christian many years, and as I think about my life, I realize God has allowed one storm after another to blow over my life—one heartache, trial, burden, or tribulation after another. Each time, He has spoken to my heart, but I have never heard Him say, "Don't worry about a thing. Just relax."

Instead, He often says simply, "Trust Me."

If I start to tell Him too many details, I hear those same words over in my head, "Just trust Me." There is something about hearing those words that brings a sense of peace to my heart. I may feel troubled over a decision and wonder what will happen next. However, when I sense God saying, "Trust Me," I stop thinking about all that could or could not happen and begin to rest in His presence and care. I also find that when I let go of my need to work something out, He handles all the details of my circumstances perfectly.

Later in his life, King David faced a very difficult set of circumstances. His life was being threatened once again. Yet we find that he placed his hope in God and not in his own ability as king. In Psalm 55:22, we discover the key to his confidence. He writes, "Cast your burden upon the Lord and He will sustain you; He will never allow the righteous to be shaken." The word cast literally means to "roll your trouble over on to God." In other words, David is telling us to roll the burdens of our hearts on to the Lord. After all, He is the only One who has the power, the insight, and the ability to handle our problems.

The apostle Peter tells us to do the same. He writes, "Cast all your anxiety on Him [Christ] because he cares for you" (1 Peter 5:7, NIV). This is the same concept David mentioned. Only here, Peter also is telling us to roll our feelings of anxiety, fear, and discouragement over on to Christ our Savior knowing that He will lift us up and give us the guidance we need to face every threat. Therefore, when all hope seems to be gone and when sorrow or sin has clouded your way, ask God to reveal Himself to you, tell Him that you want His will for your life, and that you are asking Him to forgive you, if you have knowingly disobeyed Him.

Hope in Hopeless Times

Elijah had just won a tremendous victory on Mt. Carmel. However, the simple threats of a wicked queen sent him running for his life. The Bible tells us that after days of running away from his circumstances, he came to the mountain of God. He climbed to a spot where he thought he would be safe and where he could be near the Lord. He also waited alone inside a cave hoping against hope that God would rescue Him.

What could have possibly motivated this great man of faith to end up cowering in fear miles away from home? The answer is simple and one that entraps many of us. Elijah listened to a negative report and took it seriously. Instead of trusting the One who had just worked a mighty miracle in his life, he looked at his circumstances and then believed a lie—one that said he would die at the hands of Queen Jezebel. But God did not allow his prophet to remain in a position of dismay and hopelessness long. He sent a mighty storm to buffet the front of the cave where Elijah was hiding, but the Lord's presence was not in the storm. Then God launched a mighty rushing wind to blow against his servant, but once again God was not in the fierceness of these circumstances either (1 Kings 19).

Then Elijah heard a gentle whisper call to him. It was one of eminent power, and he knew it was the voice of God. When the prophet became still and was ready to listen for the word of the Lord, God spoke to him and guided him home. You may be on the run from God hoping that He will give up and just let you lay down in your discouragement and fear, but He knows exactly where to find you. He also understands the hope you need for the journey home.

Never Forsaken

I have no idea what problem you are facing, but I do know that you are not alone. You may look at your life and wonder, "God, how did I get in this mess?" "Why did you allow me to fall to this place?" "How will I ever get out of this?" "When I look at my life, the only thing I can see is a long, dark tunnel and there is not even a ray of light falling down. Is there any hope for me?" As far as you may be concerned, the walls of life have closed in on you and there is no place to turn.

Each of us will walk through times of darkness when all we will want to do is find a cave and crawl in it, but we must not do this. All of us have wept over the heartaches, struggles, trials, and temptations that we have had to face. We did not know how we would find our way through the darkness. There have been times in my life when I have gone to bed at night wondering, "Lord, what are you going to do about all of this?" I also have prayed, "God, why don't you do something?" One of the most wonderful aspects of our Lord's life is the fact that He cried out on the cross, "My God, My God, why have You forsaken Me?" (Mark 15:34).

If we are really honest, each of us would admit that we also have cried out, "Lord, why are you forsaking me? Why don't you do something in my life?" He knows when you walk through the valley of temptation—when you want to do what is right but you just do not seem to be able to do it. You try, but you fail and then you want to quit—give up and walk away. But you do not have to give up. Do not ever consider giving up. There is something about giving up that carries an awesome penalty.

A Test of Endurance

When a person gives up, he damages his self-esteem and something happens to his attitude. Instead of life just looking dark for a season, problems suddenly seem insurmountable. However, nothing is too difficult for God. No problem is too great for Him to handle. Abraham and Sarah thought there was no way that they would ever have children. Both were far too old. However, God reminded them of His promise and then said, "Is anything too difficult for the Lord? At the appointed time I will return to you, at this time next year, and Sarah will have a son" (Genesis 18:14). This is exactly what happened! The storms of life are not confined to physical storms. They can be emotional and mental. They also can come as the result of a sincere disappointment. However, when we seek Him, God gives us the ability to do what Moses did, "He endured, as seeing Him who is unseen" (Hebrews 11:27).

There is a poem that makes this very point very clearly. It says,

Trust Him when dark doubts assail you,
Trust Him when your strength is small.
Trust Him when, to simply trust Him
Seems the hardest thing of all.
Trust Him, He is ever faithful
Trust Him, for His will is best.
Trust Him, for the heart of Jesus
Is the only place of rest.
Trust Him then through cloud and sunshine;
All you cares upon Him cast,
'Til the storms of life are over
And the trusting days are past.

—W. Cameron Townsend

The second thing that happens when we give up is that we miss out on the tremendous blessing God has for us, especially for those who are willing to undergo and endure hardship and difficulty. The Israelites had been given the Promised Land, but they did not go in and claim it. Securing the land, seemed too hard, and they became overwhelmed by the prospect of doing what they knew God had given them to do.

Instead of obeying the Lord from the beginning, they sent twelve spies to see if the land was good. Sure enough, ten of the men brought back a negative report saying that there were giants in the land and more than likely everyone would die (Numbers 13:27-31). Two men, Joshua and Caleb, had an opposite view. They believed that the land was indeed good and that with God's help they could take it from their enemies.

Sadly, negativism won out, and the people refused to enter the land. God was angry at the nation of Israel. In fact, an entire generation passed away before Israel had another opportunity to go into the land that God had given them. Only Joshua and Caleb and Moses survived. The next time they surveyed the land, they came back and said, "Surely the Lord has given all the land into our hands; moreover, all the inhabitants of the land have melted away before us" (Joshua 2:24). The first time around, Israel had missed the blessing of God, but the second time, they had learned the lesson of obedience and entered into God's promised blessing.

The third thing that happens when we give up is that we limit God's use of our lives. There will be times when the battle you face seems to be too much for you. In fact, you cannot imagine how you will make it through, but God does. He knows exactly what you need and when you need it. If you give up now, there is no telling what you will miss. God has a purpose for the pain you are suffering. He used adversity in Job's life to refine his servant and prepare him for an even greater blessing than he once had. With God's strength, Job withstood the enemy's wicked blows and the Lord was glorified though Job suffered a great loss. Are you ready to step over into the promised blessing that God has prepared for you? Or have you been tempted to turn around and run at the thought of having to endure for a long period of time?

Before her retirement, Supreme Court Justice Sandra Day O'Connor was asked what her confirmation hearings had been like. She looked straight into the eyes of the interviewer and said, "a test of endurance." We gain nothing in this life apart from endurance, which involves two things—patience and time.

Endurance means that I am willing to stay at my post—where God has placed me—until He tells me to move forward. It also means that no matter how hard life may become, I will follow wherever He leads. I will remain committed to waiting on Him for His direction and guidance.

In 2 Timothy 2:3, Paul tells us to be willing to "suffer hardship . . . as a good soldier of Christ Jesus." This is why it is critical to have a right focus. If we are worried and fretting over what will happen tomorrow, we will not be able to make godly decisions today. In fact, we will not even be able to hear God's voice because we will be so caught up in the chatter of our doubts and fears. This is what happened to the nation of Israel. They listened to the enemy's lies—telling them that they could not go into the land and claim what God had given to them.

We often do the same. A young man received a football scholarship to a well-known college, but he felt as though he could not make the grades needed to stay in the program. Even before he stepped onto the college campus, he was ready to quit. His entire education had been paid for, but fear of failure prevented him from taking advantage of the opportunity. If God has called you to a certain task, you can be sure that He will equip you to do it. Trust Him and when He says, "Step forward," take your first step, and you will see His blessing open up before you.

You may have to face affliction and persecution. However, when you do, God will give you the strength and ability you need to do this without complaining. Instead, of becoming frustrated to the point of giving up, you will be able to face the difficulty with a sure confidence knowing that the same God who has allowed these circumstances to touch your life has promised to bear the burden for you and walk beside you every step of the way. He is your burden bearer. You do not have to carry the weight of sorrow by yourself because He will carry it for you.

Jesus told His followers in Matthew 11:28-30, "Come to Me, all who are weary and heavy-laden, and I will give you rest. Take My yoke upon you and learn from Me, for I am gentle and humble in heart, and you will find rest for your souls. For My yoke is easy and My burden is light." We are the ones who make sorrow and heartache even more difficult to bear. Many times, we believe Satan's lies. Problems arise and we immediately think that life is over or that we will never be able to rebound from our problems. Nothing, however, is impossible with God (Matthew 19:26).

Five Principles That Lead to Victory

There are five principles that will help you turn away from the temptation to give up. They also help you understand how to trust God even when it seems that there is no end in sight to the trouble you are experiencing.

• *Stop focusing on your circumstances and begin focusing on the promises of God.* The night that Jesus walked across a stormy sea to the boat carrying His Disciples, Peter shouted out to the Lord, "Lord, if it is You,

command me to come to You on the water" (Matthew
14:28). Jesus told him to "come," and Peter got out of the
boat and began to walk to the Savior. However, halfway
there he began to notice the strength of the wind and the
height of the waves and before he knew it, he was sinking
and crying out to Jesus for help.

The Lord reached down and saved him. Then He said,
"You of little faith, why did you doubt?" (v. 31). We can
almost hear Jesus' words to His disappointed disciple, "You
were doing so good. Why did you stop? You would have
made it, but you took your eyes off of Me and began to
worry about the storm that was around you. Do you not
know that I am your peace in time of difficulty and
trouble?"

When he was fifty-five years old, J. C. Penny was
tempted to think that his life was over. He was in terrible
health along with being seven million dollars in debt. He
could have said, "I give up. I quit. I declare bankruptcy."
However, he refused to focus on his circumstances.
Instead, he majored on the possibilities, and by the time he
was ninety years old, he had not only regained what he had

lost, he was the head of one of our country's largest retailers—one that continues to bear his name today.

You may feel as though you just want to give up, but giving up is easy. Anyone can quit and walk away from life. However, it takes courage to go on when it appears that every avenue has been blocked and every opportunity removed. The pathway to hope and victory often runs straight through the valley of adversity—one that is difficult and full of heartache, affliction, and suffering. The key to endurance is not found in running to this friend and then another for advice. It is only found at the feet of Jesus, where we also learn to say no to discouragement and yes to God. After all, He is the One who knows you by name and has a marvelous plan for your life.

• *Be willing to make a commitment not to give up.* Only Jesus Christ suffered more than Job did. Job was God's man and Satan knew it. He also was sure that Job would fail the test. This is why he requested an opportunity to test his faithfulness. God allowed it and in the heat of the adversity when it appeared that his misery could not become worse, Job declared his faith in God. "Though He slay me, I will hope in Him" (Job 13:15).

After Christ's death, the disciples were full of fear and discouragement. In fact, even after they had seen the Lord, they continued to wonder what they would do. Finally, they returned to their old jobs as fishermen. When Jesus found them one morning, they were on the Sea of Galilee throwing nets out into the water. Weeks earlier, they were His disciples, following Him throughout the countryside, listening to Him teach, and being trained to minister His truth to others. Then the dream appeared to fall apart. From their perspective the goal became unreachable, and they wanted to give up. But Jesus came to them, and He comes to each one of us who experience feelings of rejection, loneliness, defeat, sorrow, and depression.

Once the disciples realized that nothing had ended and their greatest fears where unfounded, they made a commitment to the Lord and never drifted off course again. Every one of them except for John died a martyr's death. John was imprisoned on the Isle of Patmos where he wrote the book of Revelation.

When things become difficult, we are tempted to

think, "I don't have to put up with this any more. God doesn't expect me to have to face this." Many times, He does. He allows trials to come our way so that we will turn to Him and learn how to live this life in total dependency on Him.

• *Claim your position in Christ.* First Peter tells us that He loves us regardless of our circumstances (1 Peter 5:7). Hebrews 13:5 reminds us that no matter what we are going through—whatever circumstances we are facing, a sovereign loving God says, "I have wrapped my arms around you and I am going to see you through this. I'm not going to desert you anywhere along the way." "When the attorney comes with the papers for you to sign finalizing the divorce, I will be with you." "When your children walk out and you find out they have been using drugs, I will be there to encourage you and give you the strength to hold out." He will never leave us and never forsake us (Hebrews 13:5). You can cast your cares on Him, and He will protect and care for you forever.

• *Cling to the anchor of your soul—the Lord Jesus Christ.* The enemy may try to unleash an avalanche of doubt and fear, but when you are clinging to the One who loves you with an everlasting love, you will be safe and secure. There will be no reason to doubt or to stop moving forward. No matter what anyone says to you, once you know that God has set the course for you to travel, be willing to cling and endure, and you will enjoy His goodness in a way that you have never felt. When you are anchored to Christ, you will not be blown off course.

• *Cry out to God.* In Psalm 34, David writes, "This poor man cried, and the Lord heard him and saved him out of all his troubles. The angel of the Lord encamps around those who fear Him, and rescues them" (vv. 6-7). Peter cried out to Jesus and the Lord responded immediately. He put out His hand and pulled the brash and bold disciple up and out of the surf.

There have been many times in my life when I did not know what to do. The only thing I had to stand upon was the Word of God. There seemed to be no solution to my problem. I have gone to bed and cried myself to sleep calling out for God to help me. Each time, He has answered my prayer. There has never been a time when He failed to help me. When I cried out in desperation and futility and in absolute dependency on Him, He has responded to my plea and provided all that was needed and much more.

When Winston Churchill, one of England's greatest prime ministers, was a young boy, he attended a private school in England. We probably would think that he was one of the smartest boys in his school, but he was not. In fact, he was in the bottom third of his class. It seemed that he had very little potential even though he was the grandson of Randolph Churchill. Instead of giving up, he kept going forward. He graduated from his private school, entered the university, and then went to military school. Then he served in the British army in India and Africa before becoming Prime Minister and was one of the masterminds behind the allied victory in Europe during World War II.

Years later, he accepted a speaking engagement at his old school. The day before he arrived the headmaster called all the students together and told them, "Tomorrow, the Prime Minister is coming to speak. He is the most eloquent man in our country. Therefore, I want you to take very good notes. I don't want you to miss a single word that he has to say because this is going to be one of those once in a life-time opportunities."

Everyone was excited and full of anticipation. When the five-foot, five-inch Prime Minister walked into the hushed auditorium, every eye in the room was focused on him. Finally, after the principal gave a tremendous and beautiful oration about all of Churchill's accomplishments, the Prime Minister stood up, walked up to the podium and said these words, "Gentlemen, never give up! Never give up! Never give up! Never, never, never, never!" Then he walked back to his chair and sat down.

There is *never* a time when God gives up on us. His eternal hope is ours along with the faith we need to hold out during seasons of great difficulty. Moses endured as one seeing God. When we learn to do the same, temptation may come, but we will not yield to its pull.

Put your faith, hope, and trust in God. Do not look at your circumstances. Commit yourself to doing what He requires of you. Cling to the promises in His Word. Then when desperation pulls at your heart, you can cry out to Him knowing that He hears your every word and He will answer and provide the encouragement you need to hold out in the face of adversity.

CHAPTER THREE

God Has an Answer for Your Need

When the world around you is unraveling, it is hard to imagine being still and trusting God. Yet, this is exactly what He wants us to do. In Luke, Jesus comforts those who are worried about the future. "Do not be afraid, little flock, for your Father has chosen gladly to give you the kingdom" (Luke 12:32). By accepting Christ as their Savior, they already had a place secured for them in heaven. Therefore, they did not need to worry about the circumstances surrounding their lives. However, this is what they were doing—worrying.

The Lord assured them, "If God so clothes the grass in the field, which is alive today and tomorrow is thrown into the furnace, how much more will He clothe you? You men of little faith! And do not seek what you will eat and what you will drink, and do not keep worrying. For all these things the nations of the world eagerly seek; but your Father knows that you need these things. But seek His kingdom, and these things will be added to you" (Luke 12:28-31).

Just as these words brought comfort to those who heard the Savior say them, they are a source of comfort today because they remind us that God is not distant and has not forgotten His promises to us. He is a personal God who is aware of every need we have. He also knows when these needs should be addressed. Many people today spend a great deal of time worrying about the future. The news media does their part in fueling the unrealistic fears of those who stay glued to their televisions. Their eyes become focused on predictions and events that have nothing to do with God's amazing ability to provide for His children.

The Reasons for Problems and Trials

When was the last time you heard a news reporter look directly into the camera and remind you to trust God and believe in His ability to provide for the needs you have. More than likely this will never happen during todays news programs! This is because we are living in a system that is not operating according to the principles of God's Word. Therefore, each morning as we get up, we need to put on God's armor as Paul outlined in Ephesians 6, and we need to set aside some time to read His Word and pray. Far too often, people get up, rush to put on the coffee and then turn on the television to see what is happening in the world. I can tell you that what you will hear ninety percent of the time will be negative. Satan is the prince of this world, and he definitely influences what is broadcast each day.

However, the ultimate control of this world belongs to God. He is infinite in knowledge. This means He knows all things. He is all-powerful and the One who is in charge of this world and our lives. Anything that touches our lives has to pass through Him before it gets to us. Nothing happens without His full knowledge. And nothing is too great or too small for Him to handle. The very fact that the check you thought would come on Monday has not arrived concerns Him, but there are times when He allows us to wait for His answer a little longer than we would choose. The fact is: God allows problems and difficulty for several reasons.

    • *Our priorities get out of line, and He wants to show*

us how to readjust them. Jesus told his followers, "Do not worry about your life" (Luke 12:22). Many of the people did not know He was the Messiah. Therefore, they believed that they had a good reason to become worried. They lived in a time that was full of turmoil. The Roman government kept a tight rule on their lives, and it was hard to make a good living. The taxes were high and the political oppression was great. Certainly, many of us can identify with the needs these people had, but Jesus is the Prince of Peace. One of His first goals in coming to earth was to offer peace to our tired and troubled hearts and minds.

Instead of worrying and becoming fretful about our circumstances, Jesus wants us to place our trust in Him and allow Him to interject His peace and assurance into our circumstances. However, today, many people are living lives that are far from what God planned for them. They are entrapped by sin and spend most of their time trying to justify the lifestyle they have chosen. True peace cannot come to the person who has not surrendered his or her life to the Lord. We can try to make the broken pieces fit, but they never will until our hearts are fully His.

Once we understand that God is never out of control no matter how dark or stormy life becomes, we will begin to see life differently. After all, the birds of the air never toil or worry. They are not pecking around on the ground frantically thinking that what they are eating could be their very last meal. Instead, they get up each day knowing they will find exactly what they need. In this passage in Luke, Jesus is simply saying that if this is true for the most insignificant creature, then it is certainly true for us—people who were created in the image of God for His fellowship, glory, and friendship.

As we watched the victims of Hurricane Katrina in the days following the storm, we found that people opened their hearts and gave in a greater way than ever before. At some point, however, human funds stop, but God's concern never does. His resources never dry up. There is always abundance in His presence.

The key to gaining this is a matter of focus and discipline. Jesus said, "Seek his [God's] kingdom, and these things will be added to you" (Luke 12:31). In other words, get your priorities straight. Set the focus of your heart on the things of God and stop worrying about having more of everything. God always gives good gifts to His children, but you must learn to wait in His presence trusting that whatever need you have, He will supply.

• *God allows adversity to touch our lives so that we will turn to Him.* Nothing gets our attention any quicker than adversity. Nothing has the power to threaten our sense of peace and joy the way tribulation does. Many times, God uses difficulty and heartache to draw us back to Himself and to make us aware of His intimate love. He enjoys our company and wants to build a personal relationship with us.

Perhaps you have drifted spiritually and no longer take time to pray and worship Him. This may have not been the case a few years ago when you were a younger Christian. In fact, you prayed, read your Bible, and were overcome with joy at the many ways He was working in your life. However, as you began to grow in your faith, you became distracted by Satan's lie telling you that you really did not have to seek God in trivial matters.

Instead, you believed that you could make decisions on your own. This is when you began to drift in your devotion to Christ. Before you knew it, you were operating in your own strength—doing whatever you felt would be right and not considering God's specific plan for your life. Problems began to grow and soon you were weary and confused not knowing which way to turn. The distance that has grown between you and the Lord may seem many miles wide, but it is not. He is just waiting for you to call out to Him. When you do, He will answer. A primary reason God permits adversity is to draw you back to Himself—close to His side because He loves you and knows that if you keep going, you will experience even greater heartache and hurt.

• *God uses adversity to purify us and prepare us for greater service.* When he was sixteen, David was anointed king of Israel. He was not afraid to demonstrate His love *greater service.* When he was sixteen, David was anointed king of Israel. He was not afraid to demonstrate His love and loyalty to the Lord. In fact, he wrote most of the book of Psalms.

Yet, David spent years waiting to assume the position that God had given him. Why did it take so long for God to clear the way for David? The reason is this: we learn some of our greatest lessons in time of adversity. This is where God sifts us for service and purifies us for the work He wants us to do.

When it comes to playing the piano, even those who truly are gifted with this talent must spend hours practicing scales and going over the material they will perform. The same is true in the area of sports. Tiger Woods and Michael Vick are gifted athletes, but they did not rise to their positions without spending many hours in strenuous and difficult training. Because of the commitment and effort involved, many people give up before they achieve their goals. They fail to see how difficulty and hardship is preparing them for the blessings that will ultimately come their way.

David did not miss this principle. He stayed the course and God rewarded him by fulfilling the promises that He had made to His servant. In 1 Samuel, we find that he was the only one in the camp of Saul's army who refused to cower in the presence of Goliath. The Philistines defied the army of Israel by shouting, "Give me a man that we may fight together" (1 Samuel 17:10).

When he realized that no one was going to put an end to the madness the Philistines were creating, David concluded that he must fight the warrior Goliath. His entire focus was exactly were it needed to be—on God—the Person who could give him the strength he needed for battle and for victory. David killed Goliath and Israel gained a mighty victory. It was the beginning of his finest hour, but it also was the beginning of Saul's jealousy over the zeal and magnitude of David's love and respect for God. Many times, we face adversity as a result of a godly decision we have made. If this is the case in your life, then you can be certain that God will give you the strength to endure the conflict you are facing.

Although David was the anointed king, God did not immediately place him on the throne. It was the winds of adversity blowing hard against his life that the Lord used to prepare him for the role he would play later in the nation's history. Painfully, he left his home and family and lived life on the run—hiding from a man who was determined to take his life. Saul wanted to destroy David, and for fifteen years he carried out one threat after another, but God protected

His servant. These were stormy, stormy times, and I wonder how many times David asked, "Lord, didn't the prophet Samuel anoint me king?"

Think about the sorrow he felt and all the times he experienced feelings of loneliness and isolation. If you were in David's shoes, what would you have done? Would you have given up, especially since God's promise did not unfold immediately? David refused to do this.

Though there were times when the nights were dark and fear encompassed his heart, he remained steady in his faith toward God. In Acts 13:22, God calls David a man after His own heart—"I have found David the son of Jesse, a man after My heart, who will do my will." What is the focus of your heart? Are you fixated on the details of your life or are you focused on God and His will and provision for your life. If the wind and the rain have your attention, then you will struggle because you will not have a strong sense of who God is or of His great love for you. Oswald Chambers reminds us, "Kept by the power of God—this is our only safety."

• *God uses adversity to conform us to His image.* It is

hard to imagine how we can learn to think like God, but we can. We never will have His infinite knowledge, but we can learn to think and reason with His perspective in mind. However, it takes discipline. In the eye of a storm, you may even conclude that you will make it through the difficulty because God is with you. However, a few days later, you find that your faith has dwindled, and you feel helpless and not able to continue.

Tragedies like category five hurricanes can come and go in a matter of days, but the aftermath lingers for months and even years. In fact, years after hurricane Andrew swept over the southern tip of Florida, the destruction was still evident. Countless houses remained abandoned and uninhabitable. The effects of a loved one's death, a difficult divorce, and sudden disappointment can linger for a long time causing us to doubt ourselves and also the goodness of God, especially if we fail to maintain a strong relationship with Him and with other believers, who know how to encourage and motivate us to keep going.

In Mark 8:45-52—when the disciples thought their lives were about to end, they cried out in hopelessness.

They were certain that all was lost. Maybe you have felt this same way. One day, life seemed bright and even perfect, then suddenly a storm erupted, and you fell into hopeless despair.

When they pushed away from the shoreline and raised their sails, no one was thinking about having to face adversity. Jesus had sent them on ahead with the promise that He would join them later. As they settled down in the boat and talked about the day's activities they may have noticed a chilling wind beginning to blow. Still, no one became alarmed until they looked up and saw the thick, dark clouds building overhead.

F. B. Meyer tells us "A storm is the outskirts of [God's] robe, the symptom of His advent, the environment of His presence." The disciples certainly would testify to this. Crossing over the Sea of Galilee that evening, they encountered a swift and intense storm. Strong storms here were common, and these men were seasoned fishermen. In fact, Peter probably had weathered many storms on his own, but this was different and they began to question if they would survive.

Finally, during the fourth watch of the night when it appeared all hope was gone, Christ came to them walking on the water! He heard their cries. The fact is these men were in God's classroom. They were learning what it meant to trust Him entirely—no matter how threatening the winds and waves of adversity appeared.

• *God allows adversity so that we may experience His comfort.* What is the first step you take when disappointment strikes? Do you turn and drop to your knees in prayer seeking God's wisdom, or do you pick up the telephone and quickly call a friend to ask advice about how you should handle the difficulty? Without a doubt the first thing we should do is turn to the Lord in prayer. This is true for times of difficulty as well as times when we feel great joy. God wants to comfort us in our sorrow just as He wants to celebrate with us when we have experienced an answer to our prayers.

In times of adversity, we also have an opportunity to learn what it means to comfort others who are suffering. Jesus Christ is the God of all comfort. Just as the good Samaritan cared for the man who had been attacked by a band of robbers, Jesus Christ will care for you in an even greater way (Luke 10:30-36).

He binds up your broken heart and though the storm clouds may rest over your life for some time, He does not become weary or threaten to abandon you. He is committed to taking care of your needs and listening as you express the fear your heart is feeling. However, the moment you release your doubts to Him, He changes the way you view your situation. Instead of feeling defeated and as if the end is near, He gives you hope to hold out and fresh courage to face any and every difficulty.

The apostle Paul writes, "Blessed be the God and Father of our Lord Jesus Christ, the Father of mercies and God of all comfort, who comforts us in all our affliction so that we will be able to comfort those who are in any affliction with the comfort with which we ourselves are comforted by God" (2 Corinthians 1:3-4).

When adversity strikes, your first reaction may be to wonder, "Why me, Lord?" But like Paul who suffered many trials and emerged a victor, your life will be used to bring comfort and hope to those who are hurting and have never known the love of the Savior.

• *The storms of life reveal the depth of our convictions.* After Christ's death, the disciples were in shock. They could not believe that Jesus had been crucified. Fear gripped their hearts and they fled thinking that they also would be arrested.

The Lord had predicted Peter's denial, but the disciple did not believe that he would deny the Savior. However, he did—not once, but three times! In the aftermath of this storm, Peter tried to understand what had gone wrong and why it had happened. He was looking at Christ's death from a human perspective and not with God's will in mind. His denial of the Savior came as a result of wanting to protect himself. Instead of standing firm on his convictions that Jesus was the Son of God, Peter said that he did not even know Him.

As the winds of adversity threatened, Peter realized what he had done and cried out to God. His denial had caused an emotional agony unlike anything he had experienced. The mental pain that came from being separated from the Lord was horrendous. Not only was

Jesus his Savior, He also was Peter's friend.

Three days later, Christ arose from the grave. And even in the glory of His resurrection, He did not forget Peter. God sent an angel to the women who had gathered at the tomb. He said to them, "Do not be amazed; you are looking for Jesus the Nazarene, who has been crucified. He has risen; He is not here; behold, here is the place where they laid Him. But go, tell His disciples and *Peter*, He is going ahead of you to Galilee; there you will see Him, just as He told you" (Mark 16:6-7, emphasis added).

The angel included Peter because God knew his heart. His plan for Peter's life was not derailed by the disciple's denial. Yet, Peter never denied the Lord again. In fact, it was Peter who delivered the sermon at Pentecost—the moment that God revealed Himself through the power of the Holy Spirit. Your convictions reveal who you are and what you believe. When we are weak, God is strong (1 Corinthians 4:10). And when we stand on the convictions we have in Christ, then we will be able to weather the storms of life victoriously.

• *Adversity can signal an oncoming change.* Saul was

totally convinced that his persecution of Christians was right on track. He watched with approval as Stephen was stoned to death even to the point of holding the robes of the individuals, who took part in the attack. He cheered them on and in doing so drew God's wrathful attention. A short time later, the Lord struck him blind with a blinding light on the Damascus Road.

In a split second, Paul went from being a man who was breathing threats against the followers of Christ, to a person who was completely humble in the presence of breathing threats against the followers of Christ, to a person who was completely humble in the presence of God. His human blindness was a doorway to spiritual insight. Suddenly, he knew that Jesus was Lord and all he wanted to do was to serve Him. God uses adversity to get our attention and redirect our lives.

In that short moment, Saul of Tarsus became Paul, a committed follower of the Lord Jesus Christ. His eyesight was restored, but he never forgot the time He saw Jesus. His life was no longer infused with hatred; it was filled with the desire to love God and to be loved by Him. He was captivated by Christ and immediately set out to tell others about the saving grace of the Savior.

When problems come and you do not understand why, ask the Lord, "What are you saying to me? Do you want to reshape something in my life? Are you purifying me for a purpose, redirecting me for a reason?" God always will make His way through the storm clear to you. You may not understand why the clouds have appeared, but you can trust the One who has allowed them to gather.

God never wastes your sorrows. Whatever you are facing today, you can be sure that He will use it in some dramatic way tomorrow to bring glory to Himself and to bless you.

CHAPTER FOUR

The Faith to Stand

There are two passages of Scripture that God has used over and over again in my life. The first one is Proverbs 3:5-6: "Trust in the Lord with all your heart and do not lean on your own understanding. In all your ways acknowledge Him, and He will make your paths straight." God placed this Scripture in my heart at the very beginning of my Christian life. It also is one that I come back to often because it is reminds me that He knows exactly where I am, what I am facing, and if I will allow Him, He will lead me to the place that I need to be.

The second Scripture that God has used as an anchor to my heart during times of adversity is one that we mentioned earlier, Psalm 62. I love the New King James version of this psalm.

Truly my soul silently waits for God;
From Him comes my salvation.
He only is my rock and my salvation,
He is my defense;
I shall not be greatly moved. . . .
My soul, wait silently for God alone,
For my expectation is from Him.
He only is my rock and my salvation;
He is my defense;
I shall not be moved.
In God is my salvation and my glory;
The rock of my strength,
And my refuge, is in God.
Trust in Him at all times, you people;
Pour out your heart before Him;
God is a refuge for us.
            (Psalm 62:1-2, 5-8, NKJV)

All of us will face stormy times—seasons when problems come, many times without warning. This is when we know that we need practical solutions that work.

I believe David was in the middle of a very stormy season when he wrote this psalm. In fact, during this time, he faced one difficult situation after another.

Most people's idea of waiting is to just sit around doing nothing, but this is *not* what the Bible means when it speaks of waiting upon the Lord. From God's perspective "waiting" is an action verb. This means it is alive with faith. During difficult times, we must trust Him to bring us through the problem, trial, or tragedy. We may think that we are not gaining ground, but we are. In fact from His viewpoint, we are gaining the most important ground because we are learning to trust Him in the darkest moments of our lives.

One of the benefits of facing difficult times with God is gaining a deeper faith in Him. A second benefit is a closer relationship with Jesus Christ. There are many things in life that you can purchase with money, but you cannot buy intimacy with God. This comes as a direct result of learning to wait before Him with a heart that is set on believing in His ability to rescue, love, bless, and guide you through whatever you are facing.

Another verse that God has used many times in my life, especially when I needed to wait for His guidance is Isaiah 40:31, "Those who wait for the Lord will gain new strength; they will mount up with wings like eagles, they will run and not get tired, they will walk and not become weary."

In this passage, the word "wait" also denotes faithful activity, where we exercise our trust in God even though we may not immediately see any results. Instead of sinking in hopelessness and fear, we keep watch for God's deliverance, guidance, and avenue of escape to appear.

Keep in mind that waiting means you are willing to remain right where you are until you sense Him leading you on to the next step. It is an act of obedience, which always leads to blessing. Therefore, waiting involves an active faith. It does not mean running from one place to another in an effort to change your circumstances. It means staying put as a silent confession whereby you declare to God that you are not going to move an inch until He tells you to move. This type of faith involves believing in the One who loves you with an everlasting love and who has only your best interest in mind.

I can remember different times in my life when I have discussed waiting upon the Lord with other people—friends, pastors, and staff members. After a few days of waiting and trusting God for an answer, they would say, "Why are you waiting? Don't you think we need to keep going? Isn't that what faith is all about—moving forward in difficult and unsure times?"

There are times when God will indicate almost immediately that we need to step forward and keep moving. However, other times it is crucial to wait for His leading because He knows His plan for our lives. If we move without His guidance, we could miss His best and also end up missing a great blessing.

Many times, we are unaware of His leading. We get up in the morning and pray that He will guide us throughout the day. However, when tragedy strikes, or we are faced with a strong challenge, we wonder what went wrong. Did we disobey God or take a wrong turn? Learning how to face the problems of life victoriously is as much a part of God's plan for us as learning to live with the blessings He provides.

Look for His Guidance

Moving forward without His guidance can have disastrous results. In fact, this is how many people end up in deep financial trouble. They make poor decisions financially and when the bottom drops out, they panic. Instead of entering into a season of prayer where they seek God's will for their lives, they push forward thinking that they need to make some type of decision. But without God's wisdom, they run the risk of falling even deeper into debt.

When trouble comes and you do not have God's clear guidance, this is your cue to stop and wait for Him to show you the next move. How does He do this? God speaks to us in three different ways.

• *Through His Word.* The Bible is our greatest source of guidance and direction. It also is His greatest form of communication to us. Within its pages, we are given answers to every situation we face. Nothing is left out. If you are discouraged, God has a cure and you will find it in His Word. The same is true for problems with money, relationships, future decisions, and much more. The key to finding the answer to your greatest need is taking time to get alone with God and ask Him to reveal His will for your life through His Word. You can count on this: if you will pray and ask Him to guide you through the challenge you are facing, He will do it. He also will provide the encouragement you need to live each day victoriously and not in defeat and failure. He wants you to be a success and the first step in this direction is taking time to read and study His Word—His personal Word to you.

• *Through the Holy Spirit.* Once we accept Christ as our Savior, the Holy Spirit also comes to live within us. We do not receive part of Him; we receive all there is and He is our greatest source of comfort, hope, encouragement, and guidance for troubled times. As we read God's Word, the Holy Spirit gives us the ability to retain what we have studied. Then when trouble comes, we will hear His voice speaking words of direction and courage to our hearts.

After the sudden death of her husband, Catherine Marshall tells how she remained in the room with his body for a few minutes. She wanted to say a last good bye. "Shivering," she writes, "I rose to leave the room. I knew that this would be the last time on this earth that I would look upon my husband's face. . . Now there was nothing to do but walk out. I sensed that out beyond the door, out beyond the chilly hospital corridor, a new life awaited me. That was the last thing in the world I wanted. But then Peter had not wanted a new life either—not yet anyway—not at just 46. And already he was embarked on that other adventure.

"Two paces from the door, I was stopped as by an invisible hand. As I paused, a message was spoken with emphasis and clarity, not audibly, but with the peculiar authority I had come to recognize as the Lord's own voice: *Surely goodness and mercy shall follow you all the days of your life.*

"It was His personal pledge to me and to a son who would now sorely miss his father."

God always goes out before us. We never go alone and He always prepares the way even when that way is dark and stormy.

• *Through trusted Christian friends or a pastor.* Another way God speaks to us is through the counsel of trusted Christian friends or our pastor. God uses people to encourage, admonish, and offer suggestions. Always make sure that what you hear lines up with God's Word. Many times well-meaning friends will offer counsel but it is not God's best for us. Also, we should resist the urge to have our desires validated. In other words, if you know what you are doing is not in keeping with God's will for your life then asking others to support your effort is dead wrong. Most of the time, we know the way God wants us to go, but if it involves sacrifice or personal surrender, we can become resistant and even disobedient. Psalm 32:9 admonishes us to not become "as the horse or as the mule which have no understanding, whose trappings include bit and bridle to hold them in check."

Instead, God instructs us to listen for His voice, be quick to respond in obedience. "I will instruct you and teach you in the way which you should go; I will counsel you with My eye upon you," (Psalm 32:8).

Waiting upon the Lord means to pause until we get further instruction. In other words, we do not move until we know what God wants us to do. Some of the wisest lessons we can learn involve knowing when to act, when to stop, when to be quiet, and when to wait on God. Most people get into trouble when they refuse to wait. It is a very hard lesson to learn, especially when we are in troubling circumstances and we feel as though something needs to happen. This is when we need to remember that God is in control of every aspect of our lives. He is aware of our emotional well-being, our financial state, and our limited resources.

Obeying Him and learning to wait for His timing is a matter of having the right perspective. When our eyes are set on our circumstances, we start to sink, but when they are focused on His infinite ability and resources, we can stop worrying and fretting. Worry is a form of control. It shouts, "I have to do something—anything—but wait on God."

The opposite of worry is faith in an all-knowing, faithful, loving heavenly Father who has never failed to provide exactly what we need when we need it. Waiting on God involves activity because it means we are actively involved in trusting Him to lead, guide, and provide our needs. If you do not know how to listen to Him, then more than likely, you will not want to wait for His guidance and will end up in a more troubling situation. After facing a serious situation with his company, a businessman decided to sell it quickly rather than take time to seek God's guidance. Soon, he was faced with a huge problem. The potential buyer did not have the money needed to seal the deal.

Instead of waiting for God's best, the businessman pressed forward thinking that he knew what was best. The buyer decided to take a chance and make the purchase without the adequate funds. He ended up defaulting on the loan, and the businessman was stuck with even more debt. Two years later, the debt remained and the businessman continued to try ways to shake free of this one bad decision. Finally, he came to a point of total helplessness and cried out to God, but not until he was standing at the doorway of financial ruin. If he had waited, God would have provided a better way and certainly one that would have not been so costly.

Waiting on God means listening for His voice and not talking endlessly about your situation. As long as you are rushing around inside, you will not hear His still small voice.

David wrote, "My soul waits in silence for God only" (Psalm 62:1). When you come to the point where you realize your need and desire only God's help, then you will see the value to waiting and listen for the Lord to guide you. One of the most exciting moments in the life of a believer is when he or she hears God's voice for the first time.

There are many people who say, "Why should I wait? Everything is silent!" When God is silent, we need to be still. There will be times of frustration and confusion—God knows this, but He also knows that our greatest point of strength is found resting within His eternal care. If He wants us to move, He will tell us. The prophet Isaiah writes, "For from days of old they have not heard or perceived by ear, nor has the eye seen a God besides You, who acts in behalf of the one who waits for Him" (Isaiah 64:4). Most of the time, God is ready to act on our behalf. He is not the problem, we are.

CHAPTER FIVE

A Way through the Darkness

Learning to wait on God's timing and His best positions us for blessing. It also creates a sense of trust within our hearts. When we stop worrying about tomorrow, we can concentrate on God's goodness for us today. In times of waiting, we also are drawn into an intimate fellowship with the Savior. David had a deep, intimate relationship with God and we can, too. He surrendered his life to the Lord and knew that whatever he faced did not go unnoticed by Him. In Psalm 139, David writes,

> *O Lord, You have searched me and known me.*
> *You know when I sit down and when I rise up;*
> *You understand my thought from afar.*
> *You scrutinize my path and my lying down,*

And are intimately acquainted with all my ways.
Even before there is a word on my tongue,
Behold, O Lord, You know it all.
You have enclosed me behind and before,
And laid Your hand upon me.
Such knowledge is too wonderful for me;
It is too high, I cannot attain to it.

Psalm 139:1-6

God knows all about us—our ability, our hopes, and dreams. He also know the problems we face and the doubts we carry deep within our hearts and it is His goal to turn those doubts into thoughts of faith that lead to new opportunities of blessing. One of the ways He accomplishes this is by teaching us how to wait for His solution and His best.

Why Wait?

Job learned to wait. Joseph waited, and David did the same. Many times, this is exactly what God wants us to learn to do—wait for His direction, His call, His plan, and

His Word to us. But learning to wait during a stormy time also includes something else—learning how to rest in God's presence. When tragedy comes, many times our first response is to tell someone else. This also is true when we receive good news. So often, we reach for the telephone and think of those we can call. However, what would happen if before we dialed the number, we stopped and said, "Lord, I don't understand what I am facing. Will You show me how You want me to respond?" Or "Thank You, Lord, for providing for me. I did not know how I would make it through to the end of the month, but You knew and You have given me Your very best."

While Joseph was in captivity, the Bible tells us that God was with him (see Genesis 39:3). Joseph relied on the truth of God's Word to him. Later when he was imprisoned, Joseph sought release by befriending two men who promised to "remember" him to the king and say a good word for him in order that he might be released. However, God's timetable for seasons of adversity is not set to our timing. He knows how long we must remain in a certain position or place before we are ready to move forward.

In fact, during intense times, God actually settles us into a position where we must wait for Him to instruct us concerning the future. Joseph already was in captivity. He had faced a tremendous form of adversity through rejection at the hands of his brothers. Few of us know what it feels like to have family members turn against us. No matter how much pleading takes place, an unyielding relative can cause us to feel as though we are less than the worst individual and not worthy of friendship.

There is never a time that God would impose this thought on us. Once we accept His Son as our Savior and confess our need of Him along with our sin, we become part of the family of God. He takes us right where we are and begins to work in our lives to grow us up spiritually to be just like the Lord Jesus Christ. This is when adversity becomes a tool in God's hand. It is never a weapon, but an instrument that He uses to mold and shape our lives so that we will fulfill His plan for us.

The missionary that found sleep eluding her was being strengthened for a greater task. She may have cried out wondering why God was allowing such intense pain to touch her mentally, but she concluded that His will for her was best and she would remain in that position as long as was needed in order to be prepared for greater service.

The woman in Luke 8 who had been bleeding for twelve years was not only demoralized, she was entrapped in what seemed to be an endless sea of hopelessness. She had spent all the money—all that she owned—on trying to find a cure for her illness. Because of her constant bleeding, she was viewed as being unclean and to be avoided. Not only did her suffering bring physical pain, it also brought tremendous emotional distress and an inescapable sense of loneliness.

However, God heard her cry for mercy and He knew exactly when her healing would take place. He knew her by name, and He also realized that in desperation, she would seek the Savior and reach out to touch the very edge of His robe.

When faced with a severe trial, many of us do what this woman did—we run first to one person and then to another until we think we have found the help we need. But nothing apart from God works for long. Finally, when we are exhausted and near a point where we want to give up, we cry out to Him and confess our need. This is when we discover that He has been beside us all the time waiting for us to turn to Him. When this woman touched His robe, she was healed physically, but more than this, she was healed spiritually and emotionally.

Jesus, because he was a rabbi, never should have stopped to talk with this woman. The fact that she was bleeding made her unclean and yet, He told her that her faith had healed her (Luke 8:48). The brokenness of your life does not prevent the Savior from loving you. He loves you and wants to heal the hurt and sorrow that you are facing, and He wants you to know that He has a plan for your life that goes beyond the hurt and frustration you are feeling. He knows what has happened. He realizes the devastating effects adversity can have on your life, but He also wants you to know that He is not powerless. He will move on your behalf and bring you to a point of peace and rest where you will be able to sense His presence and know that He is in control of all that is beyond your human ability.

Steps to Learning How to Wait

How do you rest when everything within you is hurting and struggling to make sense out of what appears to be a senseless situation?

• *Ask God to help you understand whether the adversity you are facing is from Him or from Satan.* When Adam and Eve disobeyed God, the adversity that came into their lives was a result of their sin. Likewise, when we step out of God's will, we can expect to suffer the consequences of that decision. Choosing to walk away from the Lord and follow after the very things of this world brings disappointment and sorrow.

The truth is that every day we make choices. Some are wise while others are not so wise. Adam and Eve made a horrible choice, but if we are honest at some point, we also have made poor decisions. However, even when we sin, God does not leave us hopeless. Just as He provided for Adam and Eve, He provides a way of redemption for us. Once we acknowledge our sin, agree with Him that what we have done is wrong, and turn away from it and back to Him through Christ, He forgives us and restores us.

The apostle Paul suffered greatly but it was not because of any sin that he committed. His suffering was for a greater purpose. At Lystra, he was stoned, left for dead by his enemies, and later abandoned by many who had once worked alongside him. However, in 2 Corinthians 12, he tells us, "Because of the surpassing greatness of the revelations, for this reason, to keep me from exalting myself, there was given me a throne in the flesh, a messenger of Satan to torment me—to keep me from exalting myself!

"Concerning this I implored the Lord three times that it might leave me. And He has said to me, 'My grace is sufficient for you, for power is perfected in weakness'" (vv. 7-9). The Person behind the adversity—not the person creating the pain—but the One using it for His glory was God.

Joseph's brothers had thrown him into a pit that had been designed to trap wild animals. They also left him to die. Traveling merchants pulled him out but not to save him. Instead, they sold him into Egyptian bondage. God, however, was with Him, and even in a dark and lonely prison cell, the Lord prospered him in spite of his circumstances.

Years later, when his brothers came to Egypt to purchase grain, he revealed himself to them. They were shocked and thought that Joseph would have them put to death, but he did not because he understood that God was at work in the adversity. What his brothers meant for evil, God used for his good and the nation of Israel's blessing.

He told them, "Now do not be grieved or angry with yourselves, because you sold me here, for God sent me before you to preserve life. For the famine has been in the land these two years, and there are still five years in which there will be neither plowing nor harvesting. God sent me before you to preserve for you a remnant in the earth, and to keep you alive by a great deliverance" (Genesis 45:5-7).

When Joseph first landed in prison, he was not ready for the future that God had in mind for him (Genesis 39). It was only through years of adversity and captivity that he was trained to be a godly ruler. This time of isolation also kindled within him a fire of compassion and forgiveness. When you have faced sever adversity, you are much more ready to forgive, accept, and love than if you have never tasted the effects of sorrow and disappointment. When Joseph's brothers came to Egypt asking to buy grain, he was positioned by God to help them and ended up being the key to their survival. He never could have been ready for such a task had he not been trained at the hands of adversity.

You may be wondering why such difficulty has come into your life. However the greater question is "Lord, how do you plan to use this difficulty in my life so I may serve you better?"

• *Be willing to submit to God's time frame.* When difficulty comes, Satan tempts us to think that we need to escape the problem. He whispers words of pride that instruct us not to listen to God or follow His principles in His Word. He also tells us that we do not have to listen to our manager at work, our husband or wife, or anyone we view as a threat. Pride is the key reason Satan was cast out of heaven, and it's our primary problem, too.

The apostle Peter makes it clear that we are to be people of submission. He writes, "You younger men, likewise, be subject to your elders; and all of you, clothe yourselves with humility toward one another, for God is opposed to the proud, but gives grace to the humble. Therefore humble yourselves under the mighty hand of God, that He may exalt you at the proper time, casting all your anxiety on Him, because He cares for you" (1 Peter 5:5-7).

Paul also understands the deadly consequences of pride and writes, "There was given to me a thorn in the flesh . . . to keep me from exalting myself!" (2 Corinthians 12:7). Satan wants us to become proud, egotistical, self-centered, selfish, and desiring to become self-sufficient. The Lord allowed some form of adversity to come into Paul's life to keep him focused on Christ and not on his ability or good works. Paul was certainly qualified to do the work of an apostle. However, he was not equipped for the task apart from God.

When we think that we have all that is needed to live this life, Satan tempts us to grow weak in our devotion to the Lord. This was not a problem in Paul's life because he had a heart that was set on Jesus. He had a fixed focus and he knew that he could definitely do all things through

Christ, who gave him strength, courage, hope, and the ability he needed for the task (Philippians 4:13).

If we are wise, when adversity hits, we will immediately fall on our knees in prayer and ask God to give us His wisdom and then to show us how we need to respond to the trial. Our world often views humility and submission as positions of weakness, but this is certainly not true. The truth is that when we submit ourselves to God's plan—whether it includes trial and heartache—we are positioning ourselves for tremendous blessing.

Joseph waited for God's timing. He also waited with a spirit of submission. There are no accounts of him becoming irate or bitter over the adversity he faced. He never vowed to destroy his brothers or seek revenge on those who betrayed him. When all was exposed, he realized what he already knew: God had a plan and a purpose in mind for his life and all he had to do was be willing to follow the course and obey the One who could bring deliverance.

All adversity that comes into the life of a believer must be sifted through the permissive will of God. When He allows adversity to touch our lives, He does so with a purpose in mind. Usually, it is allowed in order to bring glory to Himself, draw us closer to the Savior, redirect our lives, test the depth of our faith, or to strengthen us for a greater purpose.

In dark times when your life seems shattered beyond repair, remember brokenness always leads to blessing. Adversity is a mighty tool in the hand of God. It also is one of the greatest motivations for spiritual growth. How you handle adversity depends on your perspective. If the eyes of your heart are set on Christ, when adversity comes you will turn to Him knowing that everything that comes your way passes through His loving hands first.

If, instead, you are focused on yourself, your ambition, and personal desires, when adversity comes, you will not see the benefit and the opportunity for blessings. You will think of it as a set back and not a point of hope or place of advancement.

You may think how can I advance through the pain of my loved one's death, or pass the thought of losing everything I owned. The scales of this world cannot measure the greatest gifts we receive as a result of facing times of adversity. God knows the sorrows we face, and He has promised to take each one and change them into moments of eternal value.

His viewpoint of adversity is not one of hopelessness and set back. Instead, it is one of spiritual advancement. "He who searches the hearts knows what the mind of the Spirit is, because He intercedes for the saints according to the will of God. And we know that God causes all things to work together for good to those who love God, to those who are called according to His purpose" (Romans 8:27-28).

• *Know that there is a time limit to suffering.* Nothing is forever and no sorrow we face is wasted in God's eyes. There was a time limit set for Joseph's suffering. The same was true in David's life, just as it is with us. You may have spent the last year wondering if you will ever be able to live a normal life again.

In fact, one young woman who was going through a horrible pregnancy and was forced to spend many days in bed when she had rather be up working, asked, "Will things every be normal again?" The answer is yes and also no. If we allow God to carry us through times of adversity, we will be changed in ways we never thought possible. Anew depth and dimension will be added to our lives. So, what we once viewed as being normal will be replaced by something that bears a greater value because it comes to us in the image of the Lord Jesus Christ, which changes us and makes us more sensitive to God and to those around us who are hurting. Because adversity has the ability to purge us of thoughts and actions that are not in keeping with God's principles, we also find that our motives have changed. We no longer think about going back to the place we were before adversity touched our lives. While it is hard to leave the memory of a loved one behind, we realize that life is worth living, and we must live so that Christ can live through us.

No one who has ever loved deeply and then lost that love, wants to move on immediately. But in time and with God's help, that person understands that God's plan for his or her life is not over, it is just taking a different path than the one he or she thought would be traveled. When we realize that God is healing and restoring our hearts, we want to move on even further than we have gone before.

David did take the throne of Israel, and Joseph became ruler over all of Egypt. In fact, in Joseph's situation, only Pharaoh was greater in power. Most of the time when trouble comes, we do not immediately ask, "What will be the beneficial outcome?" Instead, we struggle with feelings of regret and wonder if we could have done something to prevent it. Or we become angry. We do not see how God can use our trouble to bring blessing and hope in our lives through a greater faith in God.

Tragedy strikes and we cry out, "Why, God?" God tells us, "My thoughts are not your thoughts, nor are your ways My ways" (Isaiah 55:8). We may not understand why our suffering lingers or the reason the trial we are facing does not let up, but God knows. And if we will trust Him in the midst of it, He will bring us through to a place of blessing. When all hope appears to be gone, God always makes a way for us to travel. When you come to your last paycheck and wonder how you will pay the next bill, He knows and He is our sufficiency for every need we have. The apostle Paul writes, God is able to make all grace abound to you, so that always having all sufficiency in everything, you may have an abundance for every good deed" (2 Corinthians 9:8). There is no need to doubt the goodness of God. He is ever faithful, and we can trust Him to provide exactly what we need when we need it.

Are you looking at your circumstances and becoming more fearful by the minute, or are you resting in the fact that God has promised to provide for every need you have—completely and perfectly and on time (Philippians 4:19). He has never failed to keep a single promise and no matter what you are facing, He has an answer for your greatest need when you turn to Him and place your complete trust in Him.

Therefore, "Be anxious for nothing, but in everything by prayer and supplication with thanksgiving let your requests be made known to God. And the peace of God, which surpasses all comprehension, will guard your hearts and your minds in Christ Jesus" (Philippians 4:6-7). God wants to make a way through the darkness you are facing. He wants to help you solve the problem that is holding you back from being the very best you can be. The question is,

"Are you willing to wait for His timing and will you follow where He leads?"

CHAPTER SIX

A Change in Attitude

The apostle Paul probably thought long and hard about the words God had spoken to him. During a time when most of us would have given up, Paul remained strong in his faith because he had God's promise: "My grace is sufficient for you, for power is perfected in weakness" (2 Corinthians 12:9).

The adversity you are facing may seem far too great for you to handle. But as I have said before, it is not for God. Even if, your nights are long and your days filled with thoughts of anxiety and even fear as you wonder, *Where is God? Why doesn't He stop this pain? Didn't He promise to provide for all my needs?* God has not forgotten His promises to you. The same God who promised to take care of the apostle Paul will, indeed, take care of you (see Philippians 4:19). However, just like Paul, God wants you to gain a new perspective of adversity. In fact, He may want to adjust your attitude toward hardship and trouble.

You may think that the men and women in the Bible never doubted God and certainly were never fearful, but this is not true. Each one faced many temptations. Just like us, they became frightened and cried out to God for help and wisdom to know how to handle the situations facing them. Their lives were etched with moments of adversity and trials because both of these are useful in developing spiritual character and loving devotion to God.

Nothing has the ability to draw us closer to the Lord than adversity. We face difficulties, disappointments, and trials almost every day. These are a part of life. The question we must answer is *not*, "When will adversity come?" But rather, How will we handle it when it appears?" And, does God want to do something new in my life by allowing difficulty? In 2 Corinthians 12, we discover the answer to these questions. The apostle Paul was facing something in his life that was very painful. The stress was so great that he asked the Lord to remove it—not once but three times (v. 8)!

Did Paul become discouraged? No. He only became

more committed to staying the course that God had set before him. He had learned that God had a greater purpose in mind for the trials he faced. The pain continued but Paul's faith was unshaken.

A Greater Purpose

When God allows a problem of adversity to linger, you can be sure that something good is about to happen. You also can choose to approach adversity in one of two ways. You can sink into discouragement, or we trust God to lead us through the difficulty and on to greater blessing.

Here is the catch: God may not immediately change your circumstances. In fact, He may allow the adversity to continue in order to strengthen and purify your faith.

One young man who had been out of work for several months was quick to ask, "Why doesn't God open up some opportunity for me? I've prayed, but He seems so quiet. What should I do?" Just because we do not see the immediate evidence of God's work in our lives does not mean He has stopped working. God is always working on our behalf. The news we hoped to receive may be delayed.

The promise we believed would be kept may be fulfilled at a later time.

In times of difficulty, we learn to trust God even though we do not see any evidence of His handiwork. Though the problem remained, Paul did not give into thoughts of fear or doubt. He lived a life of faith and obedience to Christ. Really, everything comes down to this: do we truly believe God is in control of our circumstances, and if we do, will we trust Him for the outcome? Out on the stormy Sea of Galilee, the disciples had one choice and that was to trust their lives to God's Son and they were not disappointed.

God knows exactly what you are facing and the decisions you need to make in the future. When you feel as though time is running out and you will certainly face ruin and devastation, He is not worried. Everything is under His control and you will not suffer a minute longer than what is needed to shape your life into a person of faith and victory, especially when it comes to the things of God.

If time is running out, then look for Him to step into your circumstances and calm the winds of adversity that are threatening your life and hope. He is never late with His provision. He is always on time and our true quest is to keep in step with Him as we live by faith each day.

You may think that you need an answer today to a problem that you are facing, but from God's perspective, you may not. He knows everyone involved and all the aspects of the situation. He may lead you to move forward quickly or ask you to be willing to wait a little longer. If you knew that His best was coming your way, you would want to wait for its arrival. None of us would say, "No, I'm just going to take my chances and move on without God's blessing." This would only lead to disappointment. Always be determined to obey God and wait for His wisdom and guidance to be revealed to you.

So many people get into serious trouble because they do not have the right view of adversity and problems. When a problem comes, instead of allowing God to solve it, they strain, as the disciple did, hard against the oars fearing that they will lose their lives. Many times, God wants us to take a step of faith, but not without His guidance. It does not take but a fraction of a second for God to tell you to turn this way or another way. However, when your mind is full of thoughts about what you should or should not do, you will not be able to hear His voice.

Paul could have spent lots of time and energy seeking help and advice from others, but he knew he already had the greatest source of help in Jesus Christ. The delay or lack of answer meant that there had to be something that God wanted him to learn and experience.

God never wastes our sorrows. He has a plan in mind for every problem and frustration we face. Always remember, He is not the One who created the adversity, but He uses each one to strengthen our faith and mold our lives so that we reflect His love and grace to others. It is in the hard places in life that we learn the deeper truths of God.

Paul struggled with this adversity for a long time. However, he began to understand exactly why God allowed it. The spiritual experience he had with the Lord that changed his life. It opened his eyes to a depth of God's majesty that few people come to know. This one event could have left him feeling smug and prideful. The thorn that Satan sent his way was allowed by God to buffet him so that he would not become proud but would remain a humble man who worshiped Christ above all else. This painful adversity made Paul keenly sensitive to God's will and purpose for his life.

The Key to Facing Your Problems Victoriously

The key to understanding adversity is found by asking God to make you sensitive to why He has allowed this problem or trial in your life. Paul asked God to remove the difficulty he was facing and you can, too. But the greater blessing comes in learning what God has for you to learn. Never be afraid of what He will show you because He knows adversity and trials are doors to future blessings.

Paul may have suffered greatly but God used him mightily. Out of the furnace of affliction came a tremendous testimony of faith—so great in fact that today a large portion of the New Testament was written by him. You may be tempted to think, "How can this be true? The problem I am facing has changed everything." God knows the depth of your heartache, and He is working through this to bring you to a new place—a place of hope and extreme blessing.

When you come to a point where you realize He is working in the middle of the adversity, then you will be able to trust Him, knowing that there is an answer to your need and in His timing He will provide it.

If the problem has come as a result of something you have or have not done, then God will also make this clear. Once you admit where you have fallen, He is quick to forgive and restore your broken fellowship with Him. He also provides the wisdom and comfort you need to get through the adversity. He is the God of all comfort. He heals the brokenhearted and binds up their wounds (Isaiah 61:1). "Grace to you," writes the apostle Paul, "and peace from God our Father and the Lord Jesus Christ. Blessed be the God and Father of our Lord Jesus Christ, the Father of mercies and God of all comfort, who comforts us in all our affliction" (2 Corinthians 1:2-4).

The Right Mindset

Many people do not live with an eternal mindset. They live for today and for themselves without considering what God wants them to do. They are earthbound in their thoughts and have not lifted up their eyes to the Lord in order to see His glory and goodness being poured out for them. Paul did, however. Therefore, when suffering came he was not afraid. He did not give up nor did his faith buckle—and we can also remain faithful and strong in our love for the Savior.

God is aware of the trial you are facing. He cares for you or He would not allow disappointment to come your way. Does this sound odd? It should not because just like an athlete preparing for a great competition, we are being trained to serve and honor God with our lives. He wants to teach us to be people of compassion—loving those who hurt us—and praying for those who have sinned against us. While He never takes pleasure in our heartaches, He uses whatever problem or adversity we face to draw us closer to Himself.

Perhaps, you are going through a very dark valley. You feel as though you are alone and do not know what will come your way next. You want to believe God is aware of your circumstances, but there is a question residing in the back of your mind. *Does He really care?*

Paul would answer with a resounding *yes!* Peter would agree, he reminds us to "humble yourselves [ourselves] under the mighty hand of God, that He may exalt you at the proper time, casting all your anxiety on Him, because He cares for you" (1 Peter 5:6-7). The word *humble* is a call to become like Jesus Christ in times of suffering. Humility is not weakness. Instead, it reflects a great and unending strength—the same strength we have in God's Son who died on the cross for our sins and salvation.

Speaking of his life, Paul writes, "When I am weak, then I am strong" (2 Corinthians 12:10). The strength that both Peter and Paul are talking about is not a self-induced strength. It is a God-directed strength that comes when we humble ourselves before God. This means that we bow down and submit our lives to Christ, trusting Him to take care of every problem and difficulty we have.

James agrees with Peter and Paul. He admonishes those who receive his letter to "consider it all joy, my brethren, when you encounter various trials, knowing that the testing of your faith produces endurance. And let endurance have its perfect result, so that you may be perfect and complete, lacking in nothing" (James 1:2-4). The theme James uses to open his letter is one of submission to suffering. This does not mean giving up and giving in but standing firm in your faith even when it appears the odds are completely stacked against you.

When Problems Seem Great!

The fact is, James was writing to a group of people who had lost everything. They were Jewish believers who were forced to leave their homes in and around Jerusalem. Many had been separated from their family and loved ones. Their sorrow was deep but their hope was alive even though they faced the daily threat of death at the hands of the Roman government. Their problems seemed great, but nothing they faced was greater than God's love for them.

When difficulty comes, we usually get through a few days thinking that God will rescue us. If the trial lingers, then stress builds and this has a potential to wear on our emotions. Soon, we may catch ourselves wondering if there is any hope for the future. However, there always is hope with Christ—always another opportunity and always enough wisdom and strength to get through the situation victoriously.

God knows that each one of us can be tempted to think that our problem or circumstance is far worse than what someone else is facing. When we begin to lift our heads and hearts, we find that many are suffering and we are not alone in our quest to trust God in difficult and unreasonable times.

How do we change our attitude toward adversity?

• *Ask God to help you see the problem from His perspective.* Many times, He wants to use your problem to teach someone else how to handle difficulty. Most of us would not think of this. But since He is the God of all comfort, He wants us to learn to be comforters, too. Apart from trial and tribulation, we cannot do this. Paul learned to identify with the suffering of those in the New Testament church by facing the same and even greater fiery trials.

• *Realize the problem or adversity is being used by God to draw you closer to Himself.* Nothing feels better than a sunny day with no difficulties to cloud our path, but let life turn stormy and we want to cry and complain. Paul's greater desire was not simply to be healed or delivered. It was to become more like Christ through the suffering—drawing him nearer to God and to an intimate place where he could weather the storm under the watch-care of a loving and gracious God.

This is why your first response to any trial should be to ask, "Lord, what are you trying to teach me through this experience?" Remembering, God always sifts every single heartache, sorrow, disappointment, trial, and tribulation so that it fits your life perfectly. He wants the disappointment or frustration to be something that will accomplish His will in your life. When you begin to look at adversity this way—the way God views it—your life will change. Suddenly, you will understand as Paul did that God has an eternal purpose in mind for allowing you to face such difficulty. He loves you and though you feel His discipline in your life, you know that He is creating within you a greater sense of faith, love, and trust.

Watchman Nee believed that all the new things we learn about God come as a result of facing adversity. It is in times of deep trial, when our faith is tested beyond our normal ability to endure that we discover God's loving hand holding us up and reassuring us that He will never leave. He shifts the trial so that it fits His plan for us and then He surrounds it with His love and grace.

• *Realize that God never takes our heartaches lightly.* He knows the depth of the hurt we suffer. He also understands when we feel as though we cannot continue, but we must. The writer of Hebrews cheers us on as he writes, "Do not throw away your confidence, which has a great reward. For you have need of endurance, so that when you have done the will of God, you may receive what was promised" (Hebrews 10:35-36). The confidence we have is our position before a loving God who has sent His only Son to die on the cross for us.

Nothing was fair about the crucifixion. Jesus was falsely accused of crimes He did not commit. However, God had a greater plan in mind for His Son. His death would satisfy the need for our sin's atonement. Not only are we forgiven, we are saved through His grace by the confession of our sin and the profession of our faith in Christ. We can draw near to God and know that He hears our deepest cry for help.

When adversity first strikes, it always seems too difficult to bear. Problems are stressful, sudden tragedies are shocking, and memories of disappointment can linger, but through Christ we can face all that comes our way knowing that there is an eternal reason for our suffering and a way to handle the problem. It is God's way. After all, it was His love that allowed His Son to die for you and me on Calvary's cross. The world has known no greater love than this. Therefore,

• Ask Him to help you to respond to the difficulty correctly.

• Pray that you sense His love even though the darkness around you is painful and deep.

• Remain strong in your faith and ability to trust Him fully with your life.

• Be determined that you will not waste your sorrows, but will learn all God desires for you to learn.

Are you prepared to suffer if necessary so others may come to know the grace and love of Christ? Are you willing to support and care for a loved one who is hurting—maybe even dying? Because of God's love that was displayed for you and me on the cross, suffering, blessing, and His eternal love will be forever joined together. We cannot have one without the other.

Many times, the world offers little hope to the hurting. If the circumstances are extreme enough, there may be a spot on the nightly news reporting the tragedy. Sooner or later, however, the adversity is forgotten and the problem no longer remembered. Yet all the while, those who have been touched by heartache continue to hurt. God, however, never forgets the hurting: "A bruised reed He will not break and a dimly burning wick He will not extinguish" (Isaiah 42:3).

CHAPTER SEVEN

Lessons Learned

From A Rebel

God instructed Jonah to head east to Nineveh, but he headed west across the Mediterranean Sea toward Tarshish and straight into trouble. Many of us have done the same thing. God makes it clear that He wants us to head off in a certain direction, and we take another route! Imagine disobeying God. Yet, each one of us has done this at some point. When we do, we miss a tremendous blessing and end up in desperate circumstances. In fact, most of the problems we face come as a direct result of not obeying the Lord. Like Jonah, God says east, and we turn and go west.

When We Say No

The prophet Jonah was commissioned by God to take His Word of salvation to the city of Nineveh. However, he refused to do this because the people living in that city were dire enemies of the Jewish people. Jonah did not want God to save the city; he wanted the Lord to destroy it and all who lived within its walls.

Perhaps, you have had a certain mindset about something that God wants you to do. He may want to you to say yes to a certain job, build a relationship with a neighbor, or take a position at your work that seems less than attractive. Maybe, He wants you to take a certain path because He plans to use you in the lives of a group of people, but you are fighting hard against Him.

Money, job security, and position can be used to prevent us from doing God's will. We think that our futures may look brighter if we go in another direction, but if that direction leads away from God's plan, then the outcome will be anything but promising.

When God tells you to take a step in a certain direction, you always need to obey Him on the basis of who is doing the talking. In other words, when God tells you to do something, you need to do it because He is God. He is sovereign, and He knows what He wants to accomplish in and through your life.

We may miss one opportunity, but when we admit our failure to obey, God moves to position us back in the center of His will. He uses the forces of adversity and the power of unrelenting problems to—

- train us to do His will.
- refocus our lives so our hearts are set on Him.
- prepare us for tremendous blessing.

Turning Our Attention Back to God

Walking away from God was not as easy as Jonah thought it would be. "The Lord hurled a great wind on the sea and there was a great storm on the sea so that the ship was about to break up. Then the sailors became afraid and every man cried to his god, and they threw the cargo which was in the ship into the sea to lighten it for them. But Jonah had gone below into the hold of the ship, lain down and fallen sound asleep" (Jonah 1:4-5).

Years ago, I told a humorous story about a farmer who had a mule that he wanted to sell. However, when a potential buyer showed up, the animal was anything but cooperative. The old farmer had boasted that the mule would obey on command then he proceeded to tell the animal to sit down, but there was no response. The mule just stood looking at the embarrassed farmer. Finally, the potential buyer joined in by commanding the mule to "sit." However, their commands were met with a blank stare. The farmer excused himself and walked to the other side of the barn.

When he returned he was carrying a large stick. When the animal saw what was about to happen, it sat down. Looking very please, the farmer turned to the buyer and said, "Sometimes, you have to get his attention." Sadly, there are times when God has to get our attention, and many times, He uses trials, difficulties, and disappointment to accomplish this.

Jonah really had no intention of obeying God. In fact, once the winds picked up and the storm clouds gathered, he headed inside and down into the bottom of the ship so he did not have to witness what was taking place on deck. When the captain realized that the prophet was hiding out below, he wondered how a man of God could simply walk away knowing that danger was right before them (Jonah 1:6).

Meanwhile, the crew was up on deck casting lots to see who was the one responsible for the horrendous storm and "the lot fell on Jonah" (v. 7). Most of us know the rest of the story. Jonah surfaced and seeing what was taking place, knew that his days of running away from God were over.

The Lord had used adversity to get his attention. God always knows exactly what to do to get our focus on His will. Jonah instructed the men to throw him overboard and into the raging sea. When they did, the waters immediately grew calm. God had Jonah right where He wanted him—in a position of humble surrender. The Lord sent a large fish or whale to swallow His prophet and then to carry him back to land. Jonah had plenty of time (three days) to think about his life and role as God's prophet. From the belly of the whale he prayed, "I called out of my distress to the Lord, and He answered me. I cried for help from the depth of Sheol; You heard my voice. For You had cast me into the deep, into the heart of the seas, and the current engulfed me. All Your breakers and billows passed over me. So, I said, 'I have been expelled from Your sight.

"Nevertheless I will look again toward Your holy temple. . . . You have brought up my life from the pit, O Lord my God. While I was fainting away, I remembered the Lord. And my prayer came to You, into Your holy temple. Those who regard vain idols forsake their faithfulness, but I will sacrifice to You with the voice of thanksgiving that which I have vowed I will pay salvation is from the Lord" (Jonah 2:1-9). When Jonah surrendered to God's will and admitted his failure to obey the Lord, God commanded the whale to deposit him on dry land pointed in the direction of Nineveh.

Then we read "the word of the Lord came to Jonah the second time, saying 'Arise, go to Nineveh . . . and proclaim to it the proclamation which I am going to tell you'" (Jonah 3:1-2). This time, Jonah obeyed God by preaching His word to the people living in the city of Nineveh. They heard God's truth and turned away from evil.

Getting Back on Track

In his rebellion, Jonah realized that God was serious. He had chosen him for a particular task and to continue to say no would be a deadly decision. Many times, God may not actually take our lives, but He certainly knows how to set us aside for a season of time until we are ready to listen and obey.

Most of us know when we are doing the opposite of God's will. We feel uncomfortable and restless. We may not sleep well or we watch as our finances dwindle. There are countless ways for God to get our attention and each one has the ability to produce enough stress to bring us to a point where we are ready to do whatever He wants us to do. He may want to restore a relationship that has been severed, or lead us to a place where we can finally sense His peace overflowing in our lives. He allows the winds of adversity to blow until we are knocked down and He has our attention. It is at this point—the point of surrender—when we begin to advance through the problem or difficulty.

One of the ways God solves our problems is by teaching us to listen for His corrective voice pointing out where we have taken a wrong turn. In Psalm 25, we discover that David is under extreme pressure. He had sinned against God and guilt was eating him alive. He longed to experience the Lord's forgiveness and restoration. "To You, O Lord, I lift up my soul. O my God, in You I trust, do not let me be ashamed; do not let my enemies exult over me. . . . Make me know Your ways, O Lord. Teach me Your paths. Lead me in Your truth and teach me, for You are the God of my salvation; . . . Do not remember the sins of my youth or my transgressions; according to Your lovingkindness remember me. For Your goodness' sake, O Lord" (Psalm 25:1-7).

All adversity, every problem you face, is a gift of love given to you from the hand of God. Whether you have followed the way of Jonah or not, adversity trains you to worship God and to long for time alone in His presence. His ultimate purpose for allowing trouble and disappointment is to—

• *Conform us to the image of His Son and prepare us to do His work in our homes, businesses, churches, and communities.* When the eyes of our hearts are set on doing only what we want to do, then we will not be able to hear God. Remember Jesus took time to be alone with the Father. He did not do this to impress the disciples, He did it because He wanted to be just like His heavenly Father. The pressures of His world were just as great as they are in ours. Christ knew that to be like God, He had to spend time with Him. This is even truer for us. We may be saved by His grace, but we must conform to His image before we can reflect His love, grace, and mercy to others.

• *Remind us of His great love for us.* God loves us with an everlasting love. It is a love that is eternal and cannot be changed. God does not love us one day and then forget about us the next. He loves when we are following Him and even when we get off course through sin and disobedience. Adversity is the tool He uses to guide us back to Himself and to get our attention when we have gone our own way. Just as we discipline our children when they do wrong, God disciplines us.

• *Provide an opportunity for self-examination.* The winds of adversity reveal the real person you are inside. When life is going well you will never stop to think, "Is anything wrong with what I am doing?"

Most people think the opposite. If all is going well then God must be pleased with them. However, when the bottom drops out of life and problems begin to appear, we are much more likely to stop and ask, "Lord, show me if there is anything within me that is not pleasing to You." At times, God allows the winds of adversity to blow long enough and strong enough until we are driven to examine what we are doing.

When we are being buffeted by adversity, one of the most natural things for you to do is to examine your heart to see if you are right before the Lord. "God am I in Your will, or have I taken a step in the wrong direction? If the problem is not the result of sin, then are You trying to show me something?"

God deals with root attitudes buried deep inside of us. Many of these have been in our lives since we were young. Those predetermined, pre-programmed attitudes often deal with our self-esteem and attitudes toward others. We may confess the problem, admit the sin, but this will not take care of it. God wants to change us so that our lives reflect His grace and mercy to others. He begins the process of sweeping our hearts clean.

If you respond to the situation and God the right way, He will reveal where you have taken a wrong turn. Or, if the problem has come as a natural result of life's sorrows and trials, He will give you the strength and wisdom you need to get through the difficulty.

Regardless of the reason, the moment you cry out to God with an open and willing heart, He moves to comfort, encourage, and guide you. Remember the intensity of His adversity is always limited to your capacity to bear it. He will never send adversity into your life and break your spirit. He will never use trouble or heartache to destroy you. He may use these to gain your love and attention, but in doing so, He always is working behind the scenes to build you up and bring you to a point where your life can be used for His maximum potential.

• *Adversity is a tool that God uses to shape your life.* It can be His greatest motivation for our spiritual growth, or it can be the deadliest means of discouraging us, throwing us into despair and sometimes even into depression. It will affect us one way or another.

The way to overcoming problems and tribulations victoriously is found in our response to our difficulties. It is crucial for us to respond to the difficult seasons of life with the right attitude. God never said we would enjoy heartache or sorrow. However, He did tell us in Romans 8:28 that He would work all things together for our good and His glory. This means that even when we refuse to obey Him, once we have confessed our disobedience and asked Him to forgive us, He will do just that and also restore our fellowship with Him.

If you are going through a dark time, when problems are stacked on every side, then you know that God is on the move in your life and He has a great reward waiting for you when you yield your heart and life to Him.

CHAPTER EIGHT

God's Purpose For Adversity

The young man was frustrated and watched closely for my response. Moments earlier, I had explained how God teaches us some of His greatest lessons in times of adversity. "But isn't there another way?" he asked. "Why does He allow us to hurt like I am hurting? I had no idea that I would lose my job and maybe my marriage, too. Will the pain that I feel inside ever stop?" I had heard these questions before from others.

Weeks earlier, I had listened as a young woman spoke similar words. She had cancer and thought that after weeks of treatment the disease was retreating. Instead, it was spreading. "I don't know what I will do," she told me. "I never planned for this—not cancer. I always thought that my husband and I would grow old together. I would live to see my children marry and then spoil my grandchildren.

Now, I don't know if I will be with them long enough to celebrate another birthday." Her words pulled at my heart and I prayed, "Lord, show me how to respond."

Many times, we can identify with the hurt a person is feeling. However, there are other times when we simply cannot. We know what adversity feels like to us, but the problem in someone else's life may seem too great, the hurt too deep, and the sorrow too intense. Still, there is a common thread that runs through the very core of every problem we face. It is a desperate need to know that God understands and He hears our prayers. We may not have a serious illness, but more than likely, we know what it feels like to face a difficulty that seems both overwhelming and debilitating. Therefore, when you see someone who is hurting, ask God to give you the wisdom you need to respond with compassion and understanding.

In Psalm 18, the psalmist writes, "The Lord is my rock and my fortress and my deliverer. My God, my rock, in whom I take refuge; My shield and the horn of my salvation, my stronghold. I call upon the Lord, who is worthy to be praised. . . . In my distress I called upon the

Lord, and cried to my God for help; He heard my voice out of His temple, and my cry for help before Him came into His ears" (Psalm 18:2-3; 6). God is our comforter in times of trial and sorrow. He is our refuge and strength when we feel as though we cannot face another trying day. He is our protection when problems grow too large for us to handle, and He is our shield and our deliverer. There is no reason for us to be fearful because He is with us at every moment and at every turn. He is sovereign. This means that He has full knowledge of the problem or sorrow that we are facing, and He is all-powerful—nothing is beyond His ability to heal or restore.

Believe in God's Ability

In Luke, we read how Jairus, an official of the synagogue, came to Jesus seeking healing for his twelve-year old daughter. The Savior agreed to go with the man to his home to see the little girl. When Jesus and His disciples arrived at Jairus's house, they saw people weeping and overcome with sorrow. Immediately, the Lord sought to assure them that the little girl was not dead. She was sleeping (see Luke 8:52).

Actually, the people had seen her die. From their viewpoint, there was no saving her. Earlier, Luke had recorded a conversation that Jesus had with Jewish officials who thought they had insight into God's way of thinking, but they did not. The Savior asked them, "Why are you reasoning in your hearts?" (Luke 5:22)

Though the situation had changed, these people were doing the same thing. They were looking at their circumstances from a human perspective. The scribes and Pharisees had been concerned about sin, but these people were simply concerned that someone they loved deeply had died. Jesus took the little girl by the hand and commanded her to sit up, "and her spirit returned, and she got up immediately" (Luke 8:55).

Death is a natural part of life on earth. There are times when God intervenes and those we love remain with us. However, there are other times, when He allows our loved ones to go and be with Him. In each circumstance, we should ask Him to show us how to pray and then to give us the ability to see our situation from His perspective. These two steps are essential to gaining His strength in times of adversity:

• Lord, show me how to pray so that I may know Your will for my life and my situation.

• Give me the ability to see my situation from Your perspective. Help me to understand that You have a future planned for me and it is one full of hope and promise (see Jeremiah 29:11).

We may not fully understand the problems that we face, but God does perfectly. He knows the right words to speak to our hearts so that we are encouraged, lifted up, and sense His covering of protection falling down around us. However, we must be still enough in our spirits to hear Him when He speaks.

Are you listening? Or are you still talking non-stop to Him about the circumstances of your life? In times of crisis, He wants you to be still and to know that He is God (Psalm 46:10). He has not forgotten you. In fact, He acknowledges the fact that your name is written on the very palm of His hand. "Can a mother forget the baby at her breast and have no compassion on the child she has borne? Though she may forget, I will not forget you! See, I have engraved you on the palms of my hands" (Isaiah 49:15-16, NIV).

With this truth in mind, why would you ever worry?

An Unplanned Storm

When the woman I mentioned at the beginning of this chapter told me she had not planned to become so sick, I understood what she was saying. There have been trials in my own life that I did not plan to experience. In fact, like many of you, I would have chosen to erase them. However, if I did, I also would be erasing the times that God engulfed me in His intimate love and care. I would have missed the lessons He personally wanted to teach me.

Adversity is a swift teacher, if you allow it to do its refining work in your life. If you do not, you will miss a blessing, but you will also find that you have to repeat the cycle at some point until you have grasped what God wants you to know. Israel spent forty extra years in the wilderness because they did not learn what God wanted to teach them. An entire generation passed away as a result of disobedience.

Often when trouble comes there is little to no warning.

However, there is one thing that we can do quickly to ease our sorrow and that is to roll the burden over on to the Lord. If you read any of the writings of the old saints, you will come across this phrase. It means to literally *roll* the burden of your heart over on to the only One who can adequately bear your problem, trial, and sorrow—the Lord Jesus Christ. He is our burden bearer and the only One who can help us solve the difficulty we are facing.

Peter reminds us that God has a deep and abiding care for each one of us (see 1 Peter 5:7). He also writes, "The same experiences of suffering are being accomplished [or being felt] by your brethren who are in the world. After you have suffered for a little while, the God of all grace, who called you to His eternal glory in Christ, will Himself perfect, confirm, strengthen and establish you. To Him be dominion forever and ever, Amen" (1 Peter 5:9-11 *clarification added*).

You are never alone in your heartache. God is with you. At times, it may seem as though He is not listening or watching, but He is. He knows all that you are facing. He understands when you feel forgotten, weary, and overwhelmed. When the disciples were caught in a horrific storm on the Sea of Galilee, He was with them, but they did not know the extent of His care and love for them. Therefore, they cried out, "Teacher, do You not care that we are perishing?" (Mark 4:38).

In their hearts, they knew Jesus did care, but they were afraid. More than likely, they did what many of us do. They waited to pray. The winds began to blow harder and waves grew higher and still they tried not to cry out, but when it appeared that their boat would capsize and they would drown, they cried out to Him.

Jesus may have appeared to be sleeping, but He was completely aware of their circumstances, just as He is of yours. Have you ever wondered if Jesus is aware of your deepest need? He is and He has a solution for the problems you face. In times of crisis, our goal should be to discover His will for our lives concerning the problem. Then we should ask Him to show us how we can faithfully obey Him.

The fact is in this particular situation Jesus had been the One who instructed the disciples to leave the area where

He had been teaching and row to the opposite side of the lake (Mark 4:35). There will be times in your life when God leads you out onto a stormy sea. From your perspective, it appears that you will drown. The sky is dark, the sea is swelling, and the wind is violent. You have no idea how you will survive, but God knows. He is the One who has led you to this point and no matter how rough your sea becomes, He will carry you on to safety.

What did Jesus tell His disciples? He said, "Let us go over to the other side" (Mark 4:35). He said nothing about stopping midway and drowning. While He did not necessarily promise an easy, carefree journey, He certainly said nothing about dying or drowning. In fact, He said, "Let's go to the other side." In other words, they were going to make it, but no one in the group thought about the choice of Christ's words.

How many of us stop along the way and become frightened by our circumstances? There are times when life becomes very difficult and all we can do is to believe in the One who has never failed us and keep moving forward until He tells us to stop.

A Matter of Focus

In fact, if God tells you to do something, then you should do it based on who is doing the talking. Early in my ministry in Atlanta, this principle was seriously tested in my life. I knew God had brought me to First Baptist but the climate of my circumstances was very stormy. However, I refused to disobey the Lord. I stayed the course by keeping the focus of my heart set on Him alone.

When the storm struck, the disciples allowed the focus of their hearts to drift away from the Savior. Suddenly, they were caught up emotionally, mentally, and physically in the waves and the wind and from this viewpoint, their problems appeared deadly. When trouble comes, keep your eyes on Christ. This is His goal for you in a season of adversity. He wants to prove Himself faithful, but He also wants to test the depth of your faith.

Although most of the disciples were seasoned fishermen, they became afraid. Why, because they were blinded to the fact that the Savior of the world was in the boat with them—the One who had the awesome ability to solve the very problem they were facing. When difficulty comes and God allows it to linger or threaten our existence, the best plan we can put into place is one that brings us to our knees before His throne. If we are looking to a man or a company to save or prevent our ruin, then we are looking in the wrong direction.

All the earthly wisdom in the world cannot adequately help you when the storms of life break over you. Only God can offer the help and solution you need to make it to the other side.

David writes, "The Lord is my shepherd, I shall not want. He makes me lie down in green pastures; He leads me beside quiet waters. He restores my soul; He guides me in the paths of righteousness for His name's sake. Even though I walk through the valley of the shadow of death, I fear no evil, for You are with me" (Psalm 23:1-4). Notice that David did not say, "If I get through the valley." He said, "Though I walk through." Are you walking through a difficult time and you wonder whether you will get through it or not? The answer always is yes when God is involved. The enemy may seek to tell you that you will not, but you will. Trust Him, obey Him, and then watch to see what He will do on your behalf.

There are few emotional warnings that let us know that our lives are about to change forever. We may realize that something is not right but rarely are we prepared for the sudden death of a spouse, dismissal from our jobs, or the news that we have a serious illness. Many of the problems that come into our lives have long-term effects. Losing your job can mean a serious shift in income. You may get through the initial shock, but you will still have to deal with the aftermath of the tragedy.

Although forecasters can predict the size and impact area of a hurricane, a sudden shift in weather conditions can change everything. This is exactly what happened on the Sea of Galilee that evening. The disciples set sail under partly clear skies but ended up being cast into what felt like a raging category four storm.

Adversity teaches us the importance of—

• *Obedience.* When my children were young they would ask me what was the one thing they could learn about God's principles that would make a difference in their lives. I always told them to obey God and leave all the details to

Him. I am sure they have faced many trials, just as I have, but this one principle is foundational to every area of our Christian life.

Obey God and He will guide you *through* the stormy times to a place of great blessing. This may or may not mean material blessing. The true blessings of God can rarely be counted because He places them within your heart.

• *His presence in our lives.* David wrote, "With your help I can advance against a troop: with my God I can scale a wall. As for God, his way is perfect; the word of the Lord is flawless. He is a shield for all who take refuge in him" (Psalm 18:29-30, NIV). A young woman who was struggling with a terminal illness insisted on going to visit her family over the Christmas holidays. She had been receiving treatment for several months and her strength had faded. Still, she knew that one of the best medicines available to her was the love of her family. God provided the strength she needed to make the trip. He is our very present help in times of trouble.

When Israel faced a serious threat from their enemies, Moses inquired of the Lord saying, "If Your presence does not go with us, do not lead us up from here," (Exodus 33:15). Moses knew the value of having God lead the nation of Israel forward. In fact, he wanted to stay put if there was an outside chance that God was not going to go with them. Obedience teaches us to want the same thing. In other words, we want to be in God's will and not off on some trail that leads to serious trouble and disappointment.

If you are not sure about the direction you are about to take, pray as Moses prayed, "If Your presence does not go with me, then do not lead me up from here. Block my path and guide me so that I will be in the center of Your will."

• *Listening for His direction.* There is a mindset in our world that tells us as long as we are doing good things, then God will bless us. Satan loves to derail our lives by telling us that God really does not care where we end up. Nothing could be further from the truth. While not everyone is called into the ministry, each one of us certainly has been called by God to fulfill a certain purpose. There is no greater blessing than to know that you are doing what He has gifted you to do—whether it is on your job or in your church.

Years ago, I preached a message entitled "Who's

Doing The Talking. "In it I demonstrated how we are constantly hearing different voices of reason—all which, if we allow them, could drown out the voice of God. Remember, God spoke to Elijah through a whisper and not from the center of a raging storm.

You may feel as though your life is in a vortex of trouble, but if you ask Him to show you how to be still before Him, He will, and in the calm of His presence, You will hear Him speak words of hope and encouragement. There are three ways God speaks to us today: through His Word, His Holy Spirit who lives within the life of a believer, and through a trusted Christian friend or pastor. However, before you can hear His voice, you must be still enough to listen.

• *Waiting with a sense of perfect peace.* David learned to wait before the Lord, and we need to do the same. God's timing is perfect. He knows when to tell you to move forward. Until He does, you can rest in His presence knowing that the Prince of Peace is at work in your life.

David waited for God to reveal His truth to his heart. Then he obeyed the Lord. Many times, when trouble comes, we think, "I've got to do something." An opportunity presents itself and we jump at it. People jump ahead of the Lord and then wonder why their lives are so troubled. Before they know it, they have added layer upon layer of problems to their lives that they cannot control.

Many times, this can be true of someone who has lost his or her spouse or job. The death of a loved one is devastating. Being laid off from a job we like can strike hard against our self-esteem.

After the sudden death of his wife, a middle-aged man announced to his friends that he could not be alone. He needed a wife. Therefore, he remarried and quickly risked bypassing God's best to meet a need in his life. He did not even know if what he was doing was right. He just knew that he had a need and could not wait any longer. Loneliness is not something only single people face. It is something that comes from not being at peace in God's presence and not being satisfied with what He has provided. A person can be lonely even though he or she is in a room full of people. Never allow loneliness to drive you to do something that you will regret later. God has your need well within His sight and He will meet it according to His timetable.

Who Can Identify with Your Sorrows?

God sent His Son to earth to identify personally with our afflictions. Jesus died a cruel death so that we might have eternal life. He knows exactly the struggle that you are facing. The Bible tells us, "For since He Himself was tempted in that which He has suffered, He is able to come to the aid of those who are tempted" (Hebrews 2:18). Jesus understands the temptations you face. He knows the frustration of your heart, the feelings of rejection that threaten to overwhelm you with sadness, and the burdens you bear that seek to crush every notion of hope within you.

In the garden of Gethsemane Christ prayed, "My Father, if it is possible, let this cup pass from Me; yet not as I will, but as You will" (Matthew 26:39). Just as we have done, Christ asked if there was another way for God to accomplish His will. No one, not even the Savior, enjoys the thought of adversity. However, no sooner had these words passed over His lips that He professed His willingness to obey God, "Yet not as I will, but as You will."

As we said earlier, surrender is not a symbol of weakness for the Christian. It is a demonstration of tremendous strength—the same strength that Paul talked about in Philippians 4:13 when he wrote, "I can do all things through Him who strengthens me." When life turns stormy and we cannot see the shoreline, we may not have the strength to trust God, but Christ within us will give us this ability.

Like James, Peter also wrote his letters to a group of believers who were being persecuted for their faith. They lived with a daily threat of death. Many were seriously sick. Some were depressed because they had lost everything that was dear to them. They had fled from their homes because at the time of the formation of the New Testament church, the Roman emperor Nero was stepping up his persecution against Christians.

Many times when trouble hits, we look for an easy way out of the situation, but these believers looked for a way to identify with Christ. They were so committed to their faith that the Roman government could not disperse their love for God and for His Son. The more men sought to put out their flames of love for God, the more it spread. Suffering did not quench their faith in God's Son. It increased it!

The same was true of the Old Testament saints. The author of Hebrews tells us, "Others experienced mocking and scourging, yes, also chains and imprisonment. They were stoned, they were sawn in two, they were tempted, they were put to death with the sword; they went about in sheepskins, in goatskins, being destitute, afflicted, ill-treated (men of whom the world was not worthy), wandering in deserts and mountains and caves and holes in the ground. And all these, having gained approval through their faith" (Hebrews 11:36-39).

The Right Response

When problems come, we also wonder if we are out of step with God's plan? Is sin involved? While these are important questions, the greater question is, "Lord, how do you want me to respond to this problem?" If you have fallen into sin and are living apart from God's fellowship, then you know what you need to do—ask Him to forgive you and restore you spiritually so that you might enjoy His goodness again. If you have refused, like Jonah, to do what He has asked you, tell Him that you have been rebellious and that you want to get back on track with Him. God will not refuse you. In fact, He will embrace you with open arms!

The difficulty and trial that you are facing may simply be the result of God's desire to test your faith and strengthen you for a greater blessing. If you sense that this is the case, tell Him that you are willing to remain right where you are until He moves you forward. God strengthens our faith and tests our ability to trust Him by allowing difficulty at work and also in our relationships with others. Often pride is hiding out just beneath the surface of our hearts and God knows that when He turns up the pressure, it will be exposed and then He will deal with it.

Asking God to show us how to respond includes being willing to submit to those over us with a willing heart. He always has a purpose for the trials He allows to touch our lives. The thorn in the apostle Paul's life was allowed by God to keep the apostle from being prideful. The difficulties that David faced were sent to prepare him to rule Israel. The suffering that New Testament believers faced was used to strengthen their faith and as a testimony to each of us.

Our response to every trial is crucial. We have the choice to become bitter or to grow stronger in our faith. Years ago noted evangelist J. R. Miller wrote, "Sometimes it is very dark. We cannot understand what we are doing. We do not see the web we are weaving. We are not able to discover any beauty, any possible good in our experience. Yet if we are faithful and fail not and faint not, we shall some day know that the most exquisite work of all our life was done in those days when it was so dark.

"If you are in the deep shadows because of some strange, mysterious providence, do not be afraid. Simply go on in faith and love, never doubting. God is watching, and He will bring good and beauty out of all your pain and tears." You may feel as though your life has been torn down to the ground and nothing recognizable remains. However, God sees potential even when you are blinded to the hope your life contains.

God promises us "[beauty or] a garland instead of ashes, the oil of gladness instead of mourning" (Isaiah 61:3).

For God's people, ashes are a sign of grief, unworthiness, humiliation, and penitence. They are also used as a symbol of deep humility and need. In his misery and sorrow, Job sat in ashes, but God restored all that he had lost to an even greater degree. He never subtracts; He always multiplies.

No one can escape adversity. Either we are passing through a dark valley or we see one approaching. Life is full of trials. However, it is brimming with victory, too. God uses difficulty to shape and to mold us so that we become men and women of faith—people that reflect His love and mercy to others.

Jesus knew the disciples could not minister to others until their lives had been broken by adversity. Each time the Savior allowed some hardship to come their way, He was preparing them for the future and for their ministry. We are trained by life's difficulties to either trust God or ourselves. If we trust the Lord, we will never know defeat. We may suffer at times, be disappointed, and even face discouragement, but we will never lack anything. God is faithful and He will provide exactly what we need when we need it.

CHAPTER NINE

The Promise

I can imagine dusty cracks of light filtered down into the pit where Daniel was held captive. There probably was just enough light for him to look through the darkness of his cell into the eyes of hungry lions pacing back and forth—watching their potential prey. As the darkness of night fell around him, all light was gone and he could no longer see what surrounded him, but he could still hear the footfalls of his would be attackers.

We can imagine his heart beating hard against the inside of his chest as he weighted out his options. There were not many. He could not run. There was no way of escape. Shouting would not work—it would only draw more attention, and he refused to listen to the negative thoughts that were seeking to break into his mind. Had he not been obedient? Did he not love God? Was it not obvious that faith to him was more than idle chatter? Yes.

Therefore, he was determined to wait for God's deliverance. In fact, he would wait forever if necessary for God's promise to unfold. Perhaps, Daniel stood with arms lifted toward heaven in worship to God, or maybe, he knelt in prayer. We are not given these details, but what we do know is that Daniel's faith and love for God was not shaken by the nature of his circumstances.

When Our Faith Is Tested

Have you ever been in a difficult situation and felt tempted to disobey God because life had become too hard for you to endure? At some point, we all have had our backs against the wall of disappoint or heartache. Most of us know what if feels like to be betrayed, rejected, or forgotten. We have heard the whispering voice of the enemy telling us that we have been treated badly and there is no reason for us to maintain a steady sense of faith. After all, God would understand if we protested what was happening to us. He did not mean for us to suffer, did He?

Adversity always reveals the true nature of our character. Daniel was steady in his faith. Though he had been wrongly accused, he did not dwell on this. Instead, he set the focus of his heart on the Lord. Not once do we read that he frantically cried out to God. Certainly, he had the motivation to do this, but that did not fit the nature and character of Daniel's life. He knew that God was aware of his circumstances and while he did not know what would happen next, he was willing to trust God for the outcome because he had an unshakeable promise buried deep within His heart. He believed that God would protect him even in times of grave trouble. But should he die, Daniel knew that he would stand in God's presence and see His glory.

Daniel had an eternal perspective. His focus had never been on the wishes or desires of men. He obeyed those in authority over him. However, he refused to worship anyone other than the Lord. God honored his faithfulness by preserving his life. Notice that God did not prevent His prophet from spending a night in the lion's den. He allowed Daniel to be tested, and He allows the same thing to happen in our lives to bring us to the same point that Daniel reached: God is ever faithful and when we trust Him, He will solve every problem we face.

Daniel could have become paralyzed with fear. Not only was his life on the line, should he live, his future was, too. Darius had signed a decree. The only person or thing that was to be worshiped was the king, himself. Daniel, however, did what he normally did—he worshiped the Lord and no one else. His faith was tried in the crucible of adversity. God used this situation to purify Daniel's faith and there will be times that He does the same thing in our lives. He stretches us and allows us to face, at times, frightening storms—not to terrify us but to strengthen us and purify us so that we become a reflection of all that is good within Him.

No Need to Fear

There was no reason for Daniel to be afraid. He had obeyed God perfectly. When we obey God, we do not have to worry about what will happen tomorrow. God has taken care of all of our tomorrows. However, if we are living outside of His will in sin, then we can expect to face some really difficult times. While He loves us with an everlasting love, God hates sin and He wants us to hate it, too.

In Psalm 97:10, He commands us to "hate evil, you who love the Lord." And in Psalm 37:27, He admonishes us to "depart from evil and do good, so you will abide forever."

Sin causes a separation in our fellowship with God and this sense of separation gives birth to fear. Deep within our spirits we know what we have done is wrong. Guilt builds and we want to hide from God rather than enjoy being in His presence. This is exactly what happened in the garden of Eden when Adam and Eve sinned against God. They became fearful and hid from His presence (Genesis 3:7-10). Even when we sin, God does not stop loving us. He created us out of His love. His greatest desire is to have fellowship with us. Sin is the one thing that prevents this from happening. When we yield to temptation and step away from what we know is right, we suffer the consequences of our decision. Yet, when we pray and seek His forgiveness, He offers it to us just as He gives His unconditional grace and mercy freely.

Few people have had to endure a night alone in a lion's den where the stench of death is so strong that it is difficult to breath. Plus, the lions used for this type of punishment usually were starved in advance so that they would hit their prey fast and tear it apart. However, Daniel escaped untouched. His life was spared and has become a testimony of faith—one that even King Darius was quick to acknowledge.

When problems escalate, you can do one of two things. You can ask God to give you the ability to remain steadfast in your faith, trusting Him to provide exactly what you need when you need it. Or you can become doubtful, fearful, and worried. Always remember, God is fully aware of your circumstances, and His commitment to you never changes. What He has promised, He will do.

In her devotional classic *Streams in the Dessert,* Mrs. Charles Cowman reminds us, "Sometimes, God sends severe blasts of trial upon His children to develop their graces. Just as torches burn most brightly when swung to and fro; just as the juniper plant smells sweetest when flung into the flames; so the richest qualities of a Christian often come out under the north wind of suffering and adversity. Bruised hearts often emit the fragrance that God loveth to smell."

Adversity provides the perfect opportunity for us to allow Him to stretch our faith, take us to new places of blessing, and to prepare us for victories beyond anything we can imagine. Elijah, like Daniel, was severely tested. He had no idea that God was preparing him for a tremendous conquest—Mount Carmel loomed in his not so distant future (see 1 Kings 18).

This was the very place where God demonstrated His greatest power to those who worshiped Baal. Many times, when we are in the middle of God's will and following His plan, He will require us to face a season of testing. A deeper level of faith and devotion usually requires time spent in darkness with Him. What is He requiring of you during this time of trial? Has He asked you to go to a place that seems far from your home? Do not worry. Do not be frightened. He is with you and He will not leave you alone.

When The Brook Runs Dry

At first, there was plenty of water in the brook where God had led Elijah to set up camp (1 Kings 17:2-5). The Lord commanded the birds of the air to feed His prophet.

Many scholars tell how Elijah was fed by ravens—animals that were scavengers and pulled meat from the bones of dead animals. However, without a doubt God provided the best for His prophet. Elijah lacked nothing *until* one day the brook began to dry up. Then the Lord instructed him to leave that place.

Most people find it extremely difficult to stay put when everything around them is falling apart or in Elijah's case—the brook is running dry. They grow restless and want to do something to escape the trouble. Even when many people are forced to stay in one place such as a job that they find stressful and very difficult, emotionally they have run away. Elijah lived by the brook many days before he heard the Lord's voice instructing him to move on to another location. He knew God had led him to this place, and like Daniel, he was determined to stay put until the Lord told him differently. His faith remained steady and his devotion to God did not fade. He understood that when it was time to move, God would make it clear to him.

The Lord had a greater purpose in mind for Elijah's suffering. He was teaching his prophet for the day he would

stand on Mount Carmel and face the prophets of Baal
(1 Kings 18:20-40) . He also was training Elijah to see Him
as the source of every need he had.

In times of difficulty, people may reach out to help us.
While we are deeply grateful, we also should be keenly
aware that only Christ is our provider. Just as ravens fed
Elijah, God may use others to meet our needs. However,
these birds were not Elijah's providers. The brook certainly
was not. There was only One person who could meet his
needs and that was God.

People get into trouble when they look to others to
solve their problems. God is your problem solver. He
allowed the difficulty, but He will also provide the answer
that you need for the right solution. The answer will not
come from your supervisor, friends, family members, or
even through a paycheck. Our provision comes only from
God.

Someone reading this book may have lost everything
within the past few months. You have a future that is
brimming with hope, but it does not rest in any worldly
treasures. It rests in your ability to trust God in the hard

times just as much as you trust Him in times of joy and celebration.

Far too often people depend on worldly "brooks" and "ravens" to meet their needs. This was Israel's main problem. They did not look to God as their provider. When trouble came, they cried out to Him. After He had solved their problem, they returned to trusting in their own abilities. If we become comfortable in circumstances that are outside of God's will, then they can become our security and not God. Even believers living for the Lord can do the same thing. They may become frightened over the thought of having to change jobs. They had rather stay where they are than to risk a change. God has a way for drying up our brooks in order to move us on to greater blessings. What looks like an ending to us, is really a new beginning to Him.

We may mistakenly think that if the water dries up then we will die, but this is never the case with God. His resources are inexhaustible. His love for us is eternal and His future plan for us is mighty and full of hope and promise.

Therefore, never give up. Though you may be facing

the darkest time of your life, if you will ask Him to cover you with a sense of His closeness, you will sense streams of light flowing down into your circumstances. You never know just how close you are to being released from the agony you are feeling.

When You Are Tempted to Give Up—Don't!

Peter had been arrested and thrown into jail. By this point in his life, he knew what happened to men and women who worshiped Christ. However, he had learned many lessons of faith and believed that no matter what came next, Jesus was with Him and he would not cave into fear or disbelief.

"On the very night when Herod was about to bring him forward, Peter was sleeping between two soldiers, bound with two chains, and guards in front of the door were watching over the prison. . . . Behold, an angel of the Lord suddenly appeared and a light shone in the cell; and he struck Peter's side and woke him up, saying 'get up quickly.' And his chains fell off his hands.

"And the angel said to him, 'Gird yourself and put on

your sandals.' And he did so. And he said to him, 'Wrap your cloak around you and follow me.' And he went out and continued to follow, and he did not know that what was being done by the angel was real, but thought he was seeing a vision. When they had passed the first and second guard, they came to the iron gate that leads into the city, which opened for them by itself; and they went out and went along one street, and immediately the angel departed from him. When Peter came to himself, he said, 'Now I know for sure that the Lord has sent forth His angel and rescued me'" (Acts 12:6-11).

God wants to rescue you, to give you hope, and a sense of a bright future. No matter how small or large, when difficulty comes, call out to Him because He is the One who is committed to solving every problem, every need you have. Tell Him your need, your situation, and ask Him to provide the wisdom and encouragement you need to get through this trouble. When you commit your way to Him, the prison doors will open and His light of hope and love will fill your heart and mind. He will show you exactly how to walk through each and every day as you place your trust in Him.

Have You Accepted God's Greatest Gift?

Our heavenly Father has prepared many special gifts and blessings for His children. However, the greatest gift is the gift of eternal life that He gives to those who come to Him through faith in His Son the Lord Jesus Christ. He can handle every problem you face, but first you must invite Him to be your Savior and Lord. You can do this right now by praying the following prayer: *Father, I know that I am a sinner. I believe Jesus Christ died on the cross for my sins and paid my sin debt in full, cleansing me of my sin, past failures, and guilt. I surrender control of my life to You. I also pray that You will mold and shape my life with Your hands of eternal love so that I will become the person You created me to be. I pray all of this in Christ's holy name. Amen.*

If you prayed this prayer to God, then according to His Word, you have been born again (John 3:3; 3:6)! This means that you have received a new life through Jesus Christ (Romans 6:4). I want to challenge you to take positive steps to grow in your new faith.

Please take time to visit www.charlesstanleyinstitute.com and become involved in our Bible study program. Also, be sure to tell someone of your decision to follow Jesus and find a Bible-believing church that will teach the uncompromised truth of God's Word to you. Today is your first day on an amazing journey—one that lasts a lifetime and leads straight into the presence of the heavenly Father, who has loved you since the beginning of time.